CORN FESTS AND WATER CARNIVALS

Smithsonian Series in Ethnographic Inquiry
William L. Merrill and Ivan Karp, Series Editors

Ethnography as fieldwork, analysis, and literary form is the distinguishing feature of modern anthropology. Guided by the assumption that anthropological theory and ethnography are inextricably linked, this series is devoted to exploring the ethnographic enterprise.

Advisory Board

Richard Bauman (Indiana University), Gerald Berreman (University of California, Berkeley), James Boon (Princeton University), Stephen Gudeman (University of Minnesota), Shirley Lindenbaum (City University of New York), George Marcus (Rice University), David Parkin (University of Oxford), Roy Rappaport (University of Michigan), Renato Rosaldo (Stanford University), Annette Weiner (New York University), and Norman Whitten (University of Illinois).

CORN FESTS AND WATER CARNIVALS

CELEBRATING COMMUNITY IN MINNESOTA

Robert H. Lavenda

Photographs by
Ronald M. Schmid

SMITHSONIAN INSTITUTION PRESS

Washington and London

Copy Editor: Catherine McKenzie
Production Editor: Jenelle Walthour
Designer: Kathleen Sims

Library of Congress Cataloging-in-Publication Data
Lavenda, Robert H.
    Corn fests and water carnivals : celebrating community in Minnesota /
Robert H. Lavenda ; photographs by Ronald M. Schmid.
       p.   cm.
    Includes bibliographical references and index.
    ISBN 1-56098-711-1 (paper : alk. paper)
    1. Festivals—Minnesota. 2. Minnesota—Social life customs.
3. Community life—Minnesota. I. Title.
    GT4810.M6L38   1997   96-41467
    394.2'69776—dc20

British Library Cataloguing-in-Publication Data is available.

Manufactured in the United States of America
04 03 02 01 00 99 98 97   5   4   3   2   1

♾ The paper used in this publication meets the minimum requirements of the American National
Standard for Information Sciences—Permanence of Paper for Printed Library Materials ANSI
Z39.48-1984.

For permission to reproduce illustrations appearing in this book, please correspond directly with
the photographer. The Smithsonian Institution Press does not retain reproduction rights for these
illustrations individually, or maintain a file of addresses for photo sources.

For Emily

—RHL

For Karen, Alex, and Ted

—RMS

CONTENTS

AUTHOR'S PREFACE

As winter releases its death grip on Minnesota, the state blossoms with an astonishing diversity of community festivals. Months of hard work by organizers, thousands of dollars in budgets, much planning and interest by local residents, come to fruition over the course of a summer weekend. From Ada to Zumbrota, people from more than 250 towns across the state come out to celebrate. What, one may ask, are they celebrating? What are these festivals like? Who attends them? Who puts them on? Why are summer festivals so important in Minnesota that it has more of them between Memorial Day and Labor Day than does California? What can the festivals tell us about life in Minnesota? These questions, and more, are what this book is about. When people are in a festive mood and enjoying themselves, they display an informal, at-ease side; at the same time, that festive mood can provide insight into areas of tension and disagreement. Observing both their enjoyable and their tense moments, we can see some of the things that really matter to the people that celebrate festivals.

In terms of what this book is *not,* it is not an academic treatise, an in-depth history of festivals, a collection of humorous anecdotes, or a how-to book for festival organizers. Instead, this book is an experiment. Ron Schmid and I set out to create a dialogue between text and photographs that would accomplish four things. First, the dialogue should evoke Minnesota community festivals: what they look like, what they feel like, what happens at them. Second, it should allow readers to reflect on their own experiences of festivals, of celebration, of the events that connect us to communities. Readers are invited to join the dialogue, based on their own experiences. Third, it should provide readers with what could be called an ethnographic essay—part description, part analysis, and part reflection—about Minnesota community festivals, based on field research from an anthropological point of view. Fourth, the text was not written to caption the photographs, and the photographs were not taken to illustrate the text. Therefore, it is our hope that the photographs and the text, in reflecting our two separate visions, create an impact together that neither is capable of alone.

As an anthropologist, I believe that how people play is an important way of learning to understand who they are. So, we have put this book together to highlight some of the important themes associated with Minnesota community festivals. We start with one of the most important: the return home, both in space and in time. The theme of time takes us to a consideration of the history of Minnesota festivals and then to the ways in which festivals emphasize the process of growing up in a small town.

Festivals and how they connect with communities is yet another theme, as is a fundamental element of festivals and communities: having fun. We reflect on fun generally, and then specifically with regard to a characteristic form of festival fun, the carnival. We then turn to the underpinnings of the festival, its organization. Finally, by way of contrast, we look at the St. Paul Winter Carnival.

I began studying community festivals in Minnesota in 1981; at last count I have been to twenty-five festivals, seventeen of them different. It seems to me that readers are entitled to know what brought me to community festivals in Minnesota, and how I have studied them. After all, every project is the result of motivations and opportunities that arise in specific times and places.

I was born in New Jersey in 1949, and grew up in the ethnically and racially mixed northern New Jersey suburbs of New York City. At Dartmouth College, I discovered anthropology at a time—the late sixties—when the works of Claude Lévi-Strauss, Clifford Geertz, and Victor Turner were at the forefront of anthropological thinking. I owe a great deal of my approach to festivals to their work, read at an impressionable point in my intellectual development. Both Geertz and Turner suggested directing the anthropological gaze at symbols, rituals, rites of passage, social dramas, and other expressive genres, with the goal of understanding how particular groups of people create meaning for themselves in the world, create "the many-leveled complexity (hence irony and forgivability) of human lives," as Turner put it some years later. Turner and Geertz both produced works that combined general theoretical discussions of these issues with rigorous analysis of specific cases drawn from their own field research. It seemed to me then, as it still does, that this was a compelling and satisfying way to study symbols, rituals, performances, and social dramas: to see them not divorced from social structure but integrated into living, subtle social and cultural worlds.

This interpretive approach guided much of my work in graduate school at Indiana University. Although my dissertation field research in Caracas, Venezuela, focused on social structure and social change during the period from 1870 to 1908, I also discovered an immense amount of material in contemporary newspapers on the transformation of Carnival in Caracas during the same period. Although it did not make it into my dissertation, this material allowed me to think about the ways in which political economic forces could have an impact on, and could be symbolized by, such apparently "lightweight" events. Carnival in Caracas was an event that enabled *caraqueños* to get a more concrete idea about the state of their polity than they could otherwise get. Fifteen months in Caracas were followed by a year in northern Cameroon, where I accompanied my wife, Emily Schultz, as she did her dissertation field research. I wrote my dissertation and spent some time thinking about events like the local Miss Fourth Anniversary of the United Republic of Cameroon pageant that we watched in Guider, the town where we lived, in May 1976.

In 1979, I began teaching at St. Cloud State University. One part of my assignment was to direct the undergraduate field school in cultural anthropology. The field school was started in 1973, when my predecessor at St. Cloud State University, Evelyn Payne Hatcher, and my colleague, Dale Schwertdfeger, decided that small-town festivals would provide a good opportunity for teaching our students how to carry out anthropological research. Festivals were fun, they were public, and they could be studied with little disruption.

I directed the field school for the first time in 1981, as twenty-two students and I traveled daily to Foley (for Foley Fun Days) and to Glenwood (for Waterama). For two weeks prior to each festival, we interviewed as many people involved in the festival as we could; talked to people in stores, on the streets, in the parks; and got a feel for what the town was like when it was not celebrating a festival. When the festival began, we attended all the festival events, talking and listening to people, observing, participating, and counting. After the festival, we visited the towns again to see what effect the festival might have had.

In 1983, we were back in the field, attending the Melrose Fourth of July and Kolacky Days in Montgomery. In 1984, a summer stipend from the National Endowment for the Humanities allowed me, along with two experienced students, to study seven festivals: Foley Fun Days, Hutchinson's Jaycee Water Carnival, the St. Joseph Fourth of July, Montgomery's Kolacky Days, Montevideo's Fiesta Days, the Hinckley Korn and Klover Karnival, and Frazee's Turkey Days. The 1985 field school took us to Glenwood again, to Eden Valley for Valley Daze, and to Litchfield for Watercade. In 1987, we studied Sinclair Lewis Days in Sauk Centre, the Jaycee Water Carnival in Hutchinson, and Wannigan Days in Taylors Falls. The 1990 field school was the last I directed and was a study of the St. Paul Winter Carnival. Thanks to a generous grant from the Minnesota Historical Society, Ron Schmid and I were able to go to the field again in the summer of 1991, and we visited the Cokato Corn Carnival, the Ortonville Corn Festival, Pola-Czesky Days in Silver Lake, Askov's Rutabaga Festival, Sinclair Lewis Days in Sauk Centre, the Litchfield Watercade, and Montgomery's Kolacky Days (Ron managed also to get to Summer Fest in Deerwood and Flower Fest in St. Charles). Returning to Foley, Glenwood, Montgomery, Litchfield, and Sauk Centre over the years was valuable in enabling me to see what changed and what did not.

Although the popular image of anthropologists seems to conjure up the idea of research in far-off parts of the world, cultural differences within anthropologists' own societies are important areas to explore. Small-town life, and especially small-town festival life in greater Minnesota, is sufficiently different from the life of my youth and the life I now lead that I am able to bring to it, at least in part, the distinctive clarity of an outsider's perspective. At the same time, this way of life is sufficiently similar to my own that I can see into it, and through it into my own life, in ways that I could not while living in Latin America or Africa. The particular balance between outsider and insider perspectives makes for an interesting and, I hope, illuminating tension.

The festivals that form the core of the data in this book have been chosen for a variety of reasons, some practical and some theoretical. This research has been directed solely at community summer festivals put on by representatives of small towns. I have excluded Twin Cities and suburban Twin Cities festivals, religious and parish festivals, art fairs, music festivals, county fairs, and special-interest festivals such as steam threshers' reunions, railroad festivals, voyageurs' rendezvous, food festivals, ethnic events sponsored by ethnic associations, and sporting events. These are worthy of study but do not have the connections into the local community in its widest sense that have been the focus of my interest. In urban and suburban festivals, the connection between festival organizers and other members of the community is greatly attenuated when it is not completely absent.

Of the more than 250 summer community festivals, some I chose because they were composed of events that were interesting or were organized in interesting or unusual ways. In summers when I worked with students, we needed to return to St. Cloud by about five-thirty or six, and so the towns we visited needed to be no more than about two hours away. In other years, I was able to widen the range, both geographically and in terms of events or organization. The result is that I have studied seventeen different festivals in a pentagonally shaped segment of the state that is defined by Montgomery in the southeast, Montevideo in the southwest, Ortonville in the west, Frazee in the northwest, and Askov in the northeast. I have not been on the Iron Range, nor have I been to the extreme corners of the state. But in 1986, I sent out a questionnaire to the organizers of more than 150 festivals all over the state and received more than 50 back. The questionnaire results, while certainly no substitute for detailed field research, make it clear that the basic structure of Minnesota festivals, as well as the ways in which they are organized, are quite constant across the state.

Finally, the orienting vision of this text is anthropological and ethnographic. I am interested in social context, in structure, in social organization, in how the various activities in a community festival can provide opportunities to resolve tensions and bring together segments of the community separated by class or economic differences, and in how festivals may create opportunities to separate the community. Festivals persist and people make efforts to maintain them because they are social practices that enable communities to continue as going concerns. From this point of view, where the idea of a festival came from is less important than that the idea of a festival exists as part of the cultural resources available to people—resources they draw on in order to solve current social structural problems. Nor is it enough to pay attention only to the events of the festival while ignoring structure and context. A festival is a social practice, and that is what makes it anthropologically interesting.

Similarly, it is not my job to criticize people because their lives and values may not be the same as mine, or because they do not accept that the only appropriate postmodern stance is ironic. My goal here is not to put people on display so that we can observe their strangeness, but to work to understand how they try to make sense of their lives, a universal human practice. There are distinct voices in small towns, some in favor of how life is led there, some skeptical, some opposed. Some of the voices are quiet, some muted, some brazen, some thoughtful, some reserved, and a few inaudible. The job of field anthropologists is to listen for as many of the voices as they can and to try to understand what they are saying and what it means.

Many people have contributed to the research on which this book is based and to the book itself. My first and largest debt goes to the festival organizers, participants, and festivalgoers at the multitude of festivals I have attended. They have been generous with their time, their recollections, and access to all levels of their festivals. Those who are involved with festivals are dedicated and serious, and they care strongly about their communities and community activities. It is my hope that even while they may not always agree with my view of their activities they will recognize that I respect their commitment to their communities. The seventy-two students with whom I have worked over the years have been a major part of this research, and without them, this project would have never happened. They have collected astonishing amounts of data, worked hard at festivals, and were (mostly) good-humored and serious. I would like to single out Lisa Pollei and René Doerfler, who worked with me in 1984.

My children, Daniel and Rachel, have grown up with this research project and have been occasional, and always delightful, companions at festivals. Daniel has even helped out by taking field notes, counting people, participating in fun runs, and carrying out comparative research on minidonuts.

The intellectual debts I have accumulated along the way are no less important. I have benefited greatly in this research program from discussions with Victor Turner, Don Handelman, James Fernandez, David Parkin, the late Frank Manning, Richard Flores, and Beverly Stoeltje. I would like to thank Neil Meyer for his help in responding to possible photo selections, and Violet and George Lavenda for their commentary on both photos and text. Neal Gendler helped greatly with his careful reading of the text and his editing suggestions. Ivan Karp has long been a major source of intellectual stimulation and support. Over the years, the discussions, arguments, reading of each others' work, and serious schmoozing with Jack Kugelmass have been notably important, not to mention delightful. Most important has been the unending and profound support—intellectual, methodological, emotional, editorial, and more—of Emily Schultz. Our lives and our work have been intertwined for more than two decades, and I cannot imagine this project without the dialogue with her that has so enriched me.

PHOTOGRAPHER'S PREFACE

I was drawn into the idea of this project during a discussion with Robert Lavenda while sitting in a small café in San José, Costa Rica. This was a chance to work with an anthropologist I respect on a topic of interest. We could bring together two independent veins of work, written and visual, exploring the traditional heritage of greater Minnesota.

All my grandparents were from the small community of New Ulm, Minnesota, where I lived for my first six years. Although my family then moved to a suburb of Minneapolis, I maintained strong ties to my community of origin. Except for several years in graduate school in Illinois and as much national and international travel as I can manage, I have lived my entire life in Minnesota. This project enabled me to go back and visually explore my roots. The people and places in these photographs feel very familiar to me.

In my work, I follow the tradition in documentary photography that seeks to explore or chronicle moments in people's lives with honesty and respect. My approach herein is to celebrate people as they celebrate festivals. Indeed, most of my current commercial work by choice focuses on people. My most pleasurable projects are when I am working with people in real-life settings, making connections.

I was introduced to the photography of those who first and most deeply influenced me—Erich Salomon, Henri Cartier-Bresson, Dorothea Lange, W. Eugene Smith, and Paul Strand—by the fine educator R. Smith Schuneman. Smitty personally introduced me to the late C. William Horrell, who taught so well by example. Two of Doc Horrell's photos hang with a number of master prints above my computer.

It has been a pleasure to work on this project with Rob Lavenda. He is great fun to work with and a good friend. As always, my greatest support has come from Karen, my wife and traveling companion of twenty-five years, and my sons, Alex and Ted, who often join me in my travels and explorations and even made it to one of the festivals.

1. CREATING A CULTURE OF MEMORY

Early in my studies of Minnesota community festivals, I told students in one of my university classes about a festival, celebrated for nearly twenty years, that had become the subject of a dispute. The longtime organizer had announced that there would be no more festival, but a day or two later, a new group in town had been formed to keep the festival alive. It was not clear whether the new group would succeed. After my lecture, one of the students came up and mentioned that she was from that town. "You and your friends wouldn't be too upset if the festival is canceled, would you?" I asked, assuming that a sophisticated college student would find the festival impossibly naive and really only for children. "Oh, yes, we'd be really upset," she replied. Somewhat taken aback, I asked her why. "Well," came the reply, "that's the weekend you know that everyone will be coming home. You can see everybody you went to school with."

She was right. Even if the young people who have left town to get a job or an education do not go to the egg toss, the kiddie carnival, or the queen pageant, they will all be at the festival. Perhaps standing in the street next to the beer garden or eagerly scanning the crowd for familiar faces or forming little eddies in the swirl of the crowd, they will greet old friends and catch up on the latest news and gossip.

But it is not just the young people who come home. Festival weekends are times for family reunions, school or class reunions, and visits from out-of-town relatives or friends, some of whom may be former residents. For people in communities that have them, festivals are focal points in the year. Because each person assumes that everyone else will be there that weekend, all of them make an effort to turn up. As a result, the town takes on an unaccustomed air of excitement. On Friday morning, the restaurants and cafes echo with conversations among the regulars about who is coming to whose house. By Friday night, the restaurants and cafes are jammed with people attending reunion parties, taking Mom and Dad out to eat, trying that new place on the highway.

Another student once wrote about her town's festival: "During this time *everyone* comes home, and of course, all new gossip starts circulating: who got married, who had a baby, and who passed away. You see people you haven't seen in months and spend the whole night trying to catch up on all that has happened. And every year I wonder why I come back for the same old celebration—yet I do!"

What do they come home to? Obviously, to friends and family. But less obviously, to the town itself. They come back to see what has changed and what is the same. Some businesses have closed, new ones have opened, storefronts are renovated, new buildings have gone up; but the basic urban outline does not change much, nor does most of the makeup of Main Street. The same people are there, and most important, perhaps, the festival is just as they remembered it. As the same student also wrote:

> Every summer in the first week of July we have our celebration. And I believe every year the *same* thing happens; there is a kiddie parade early in the week, the Jaycees put on a Turkey BBQ, there is a river raft race on the Rum River, all of the "carnies" begin milling around town much to the dismay of every young girl's mother and of course it all ends with a parade followed by every citizen in the whole town heading down to the carnival afterwards. Every year, everybody says the same thing afterwards, "It's just not the same as it used to be," but nevertheless you see those same people there year after year doing the same things year after year. The same bands, the same old cars, the same floats and of course the same old fire truck going by and squirting whoever they see that they know.

This predictability is comforting, regardless of how those who now live out of town may have felt when they left. If they were sorry to leave, there is at least some solace in knowing that things have stayed the same. The values held so dear are still strong, it was a good place to grow up, and they are right to be sad that they had to leave. Those who could not wait to leave are also pleased. All the things they did not like are still there, it was a terrible place to live, and they are right to be glad they left.

The continuity in festivals is noteworthy. I went to my first Minnesota community festival in 1979, and nearly twenty years later, very little has changed. The festival is made up mostly of the same events held in the same places according to the same plan, sometimes even with the same people in charge. When I look at old photographs of festivals, the events portrayed do not look much different from those of last summer. There are good reasons for this. Once something works well, why change it? The corn feed at the Cokato Corn Carnival has been held since 1949, and the way to put it on has been passed down from one organizer to the next. Everything works very smoothly, festivalgoers like it, and it has the weight and pleasures of tradition. The same is true of the queen pageants, parades, beer gardens, bingo, and all the rest.

But there is more to it than just inertia. Continuity itself is a central element in a festival. Continuity gives everyone—people who live in the town and visitors as well—a sense of timelessness, of tradition, of collective memory. Many things fragment the collective lives of people in small towns (or anywhere)—jobs, school, and children's activities; disagreements over local, regional, and national economic and political issues; disagreements over religion and education; and ethnic, racial, economic, and religious distinctions. Festivals cut across all those boundaries, allowing people to assert their membership in the community without having to disagree—and without having to exert themselves too much. In a festival, no one has to stand up and be counted or formally swear allegiance to the town. Rather, the festival encourages easygoing participation. It is enough to go to the parade, the barbecue, the queen pageant. It is enough to chat amiably with your neighbors, to say hello to people you recognize, to talk about summer plans and what the children are doing. You can show yourself and others that you belong to the town by attending and by being sociable. Organizing the festival takes much more work and commitment, but the organizers are a minority, albeit an important one.

The Minnesota Festival Model

What are these festivals that people come home to? What goes on at Minnesota festivals? There are well over two hundred community festivals in Minnesota between Memorial Day and Labor Day. Looking over a list of festival names, a reader might assume that the different categories of names indicate different kinds of festivals. Some festivals appear to be product oriented, like Frazee Turkey Days, the Askov Rutabaga Festival, or Park Rapids Logging Days. Some seem ethnically oriented, such as Montgomery Kolacky Days, Tyler Aebleskiver Days, and Cambridge Swedish Heritage Days. (A kolacky is a bun filled with fruit or poppy seed and is of Bohemian origin; an aebleskiver is a Danish round pancake made in a special skillet and served with powdered sugar, jelly, preserves, or maple syrup.) Other festivals highlight local attractions: the Glenwood Waterama, Sauk Centre Sinclair Lewis Days, Waterville Bullhead Days. Some simply emphasize activities, such as the Foley Fun Days and the Grand Marais Fisherman's Picnic. The names, however, are rather deceptive, for there is a basic festival model in Minnesota. The classic community summer festival features a parade, ideally with high school bands, and almost always has street dances; a beer garden; "festival food" (bratwurst, hamburgers, soda pop, cotton candy, ice cream, popcorn), usually sold by youth organizations or service clubs; a traveling carnival; a ten-kilometer run; and a queen pageant. Typical festivals also include activities for children, frequently contests and a kiddie parade. Often there is a street sale or "crazy days" business promotion. Other events depend on local interest, and they include car shows, water-ski shows, old-time music, art in the park, craft shows.

Some of these events are there because they are traditional or popular; others, because they provide ways for local service or youth organizations to make money; and still others, because a local citizen saw the event in another town and thought it might be fun or interesting. Ten-kilometer runs, for example, started more than twenty years ago in community festivals as a result of the fitness boom in the 1970s. Not only were many local people interested in running six miles, but a good race, organizers discovered, would attract runners from quite a distance. A friend of mine from St. Cloud used to drive sixty miles each way to run in the Glenwood Waterama race because of the beauty of the course and the quality of the competition and because, in the late seventies, the top prize was a color television. Recently, as long-distance cycling has become popular, bicycle races have started to appear in festivals.

The answer to the question of why Minnesota festivals resemble each other is twofold. First, the Minnesota summer community festival model is based on people's prior experience living in Minnesota. The model that Minnesotans carry around in their heads is probably not identical to any one real festival but is a combination of many. Festivals are not uniquely created in each town, springing full-grown from the minds of community members without reference to any other festivals. Ideas about festivals—what they should include, how they should be organized and financed—diffuse from town to town about the state. Second, because people in small Minnesota towns have much in common, their festivals are similar, too. Small-town Minnesotans participate in American popular culture (they watch television, listen to music on the radio, buy recordings, go to the movies, follow sports), they have common experiences of small-town life, they have the sense that they need to build community, and they have similar educations, jobs, and tastes. I do not mean to suggest that Minnesota festivals are simply clones of each other. The particular characteristics of individual communities are certainly reflected in their festivals. But to the outside observer, the similarities are striking.

Festivals and Memory

These characteristics—continuity, coming home, and a set of deeply familiar events—help to form a central feature of festivals: the way they create and maintain memories. As we live out our lives, we seem to move forward through time. We pass from elementary school to junior high school and high school. We go to college, marry, have children, move through our career. We watch ourselves and others age. But simultaneous with this linear sense of time is a cyclical one, embodied for many of us in holidays. Labor Day, Halloween, Thanksgiving, Christmas, New Year's, Easter, Memorial Day, July 4th—all return every year, forming a fixed cycle in our otherwise transitory life experience. Because these holidays are fixed, they are like islands in a stream. Memories sediment around them. "Remember that last Christmas with Grandpa?" "The year when it rained so hard on July 4th? That's when we first met." "It was the year of the Halloween blizzard—when was that?—that the girls' volleyball team went to the state championship." The years slip away from our recollections, but the memories fixed around recurring moments in time provide us with a way of holding onto the past and our common history.

Festivals enter into the cycle of fixed moments in time, but in a distinctive way. For most people, particularly those outside religious or ethnic communities, the holiday cycle is not a community cycle. Residents of a small town do not celebrate Thanksgiving or Labor Day or Christmas with one another. In the towns that have them, festivals are recurring *community* events, and as a result, people's memories of their towns *as communities* accumulate around festivals. This gives festivals an unusual kind of power. It is a power not so much to change social life, or to alter or enforce a social structure, as to structure people's memories and emotions. It is no accident that photographing and videotaping families and friends in the festival is so common, for these are ways to create memory. The place, the event, and the people become intertwined in the records and images that we use to grasp hold of time.

The festival provides a context within which memories are created, but also creates memories itself. These are of two kinds: memories of things that happen in festivals and memories of the physical participation in the life of the community through the action of involvement of some kind in the festival—what could be called "festivaling." In regard to the former, for example, consider what happened at the culminating moment of the outdoor queen pageant in Mongtomery in 1983. As all the candidates rushed to the center of the stage, which was about four feet off the ground, to hug the just-crowned winner, the stage collapsed. No one was hurt and not even a single gown was torn. But what a moment! That event provided those who were there and those who heard about it with a common memory that they can use to communicate with people with whom they might otherwise not have a great deal in common. At the same time, it has become a piece of community history, a social memory.

Festivals have histories recorded in the newspapers, the police logs, the city clerk's office, and people's photo albums, stories, and accumulated memories. These histories enable festivals to become a symbol that stands for the community, or at least part of it, and to become a way of distinguishing one community from all others. The health and success of the festival come to be read as indicators of the health and success of the wider community in which the festival is celebrated.

Thus the festival becomes a tool that allows people to think about their community in concrete ways. The festival can enable residents to compare their towns to other towns, or it can enable them to reflect on the community's past by way of an emphasis on heritage. In most towns now, heritage refers less to the ethnic heritage than to community history, especially that of the town's foundation and early years. To direct attention to community history is to encourage residents to reflect on what distinguishes their way of life from other ways of life in Minnesota and beyond. By continuing to participate in these celebrations, as organizer, as participant, as spectator, people make a conscious statement of their commitment to what they think the festival represents. The festival becomes a symbol of identity for them, providing a way for them to celebrate their way of life, just because it is *theirs*.

Festivals as Performance

But festivals are not just "good to think"; they are also good to perform. Paul Connerton, in his 1989 book, *How Societies Remember,* emphasizes that social memory derives from performance and that, therefore, social memory involves the body. This kind of memory comes through what I have called "festivaling." There is a sheer physicality that Minnesota festivals allow, if not revel in. The sensory and bodily experiences of festivals are both distinctive and memorable:

smelling the barbecue in the park and eating the roast chicken; dancing on the street or in the park and hearing the music; smelling the beer garden and carrying foaming pitchers of beer to the table to pour and enjoy; getting nauseous from too many corn dogs, minidonuts, or carnival rides; carrying lawn chairs to the parade and then watching and feeling, not merely hearing, the power of the high school bands; strolling down the center of a closed Main Street; getting sunburned from the afternoon in the park. These experiences of festivaling engage people's minds, bodies, and emotions, and lay down sets of physical, cognitive, and emotional memories. Perhaps one of the most interesting illustrations of the simultaneous involvement of mind, body, and emotion can be observed at the start of every festival parade I have ever watched. As the color guard at the head of the parade approaches, a wave precedes it; everyone rises to honor the flag, and men remove their hats. As the flags pass, people resume their seats. This is the only time during the parade that the movement of the people watching the parade is not random. This act of respect to a key American symbol is what Connerton calls "bodily social memory."

As performance, the festival follows a script that the participants interpret creatively. Festival events are scheduled in a particular order and carried out in a particular way. The way the festival script is put together makes possible certain kinds of encounters, certain kinds of connections, certain kinds of fun, certain kinds of understandings. For example, festivals whose major events occur during the week make it likely that those attending will see fewer outsiders—tourists— than they would if the festival events occurred during the weekend. Some festivals, like the Glenwood Waterama, are organized so that one event leads to the next, moving people from one part of town to another as they follow the parade to the city park or leave the craft show at the fairground to get ready for the water-ski show.

Having the queen pageant at the end of the festival produces a remarkably different result than does scheduling it at the beginning. At the beginning, one of the major competitive events is over before the festival has barely begun, and the losing candidates must stay around for all the events that require their attendance: the kiddie parade, the grand day parade, activities in the city park. This situation is painful for the losing candidates. (I overheard one of them remark, as she and two others arrived at a city park for an event, "Here are the losers.") Little attention is paid to them after the pageant is over. As a result, at festivals where the queen pageant is first, there is little emphasis on the pageant as a competitive event or on the role the pageant can play in transforming the candidates. By contrast, when the queen pageant is at the end of the festival, the candidates become a focus of the festival. They are seen in attendance at various events, visiting nursing homes, and doing other things together, causing people to speculate on which will win and why.

Certain events feature performance. Sometimes this is straightforward: the marching bands perform, the queen candidates perform, the children in the kiddie parade perform. But other kinds of performances are taking place, too. The festival organizers are displaying their qualities as leaders, as organizers, as people with clout, good ideas, and a commitment to the town. The dancers at the street dance are not only having a good time; in the way they dress, hold themselves, interact with others—and, of course, in the way they dance—they are making a statement about who they think they are. They are, as it were, performing themselves. Festivals permit these kinds of moments in public. After all, one of the significant aspects of the festival is its public yet informal nature.

Heritage and Memory

The choices festival organizers make for the theme of their festival result in different ways of thinking about the past and present of their community. A committee could choose to emphasize farm and town connections (as in Paynesville's Town and Country Days), to promote area crafters and businesses, to lure tourists to the area, or to celebrate a local landmark, industry, or community heritage. Each of these choices represents a different "take" on the community, its needs, its wishes, and what the festival can accomplish and stand for.

Because towns are part of a larger regional system, their choices for festival themes are not entirely free. There is an economy of symbols as well as an industrial and commercial economy. I have been told several times that New Prague would be seriously interested in taking Kolacky Days if ever Montgomery were to let it go. But from the perspective of festival organizers in the area of Le Sueur, Scott, and Rice Counties, Czech heritage is already spoken for as a festival theme, so they must emphasize something else.

Because heritage "sells," choosing it as a theme may sometimes be a strategy for trying to halt a decline in the festival or in the town's morale by giving people something to be involved in and proud of, reengaging them in the life of the town. In this way, choosing heritage ironically becomes a way of choosing change rather than the status quo.

By choosing, festival organizers close off other options. To choose heritage, for example, is to exclude or downplay other ways of thinking about the community's present regional economic and political system, about the town's relations with rural people, about the needs of the present and possibilities for the future.

It implies that the image of the isolated community with its rural area, independent and autonomous, is realistic and that the old ways of dealing with life were good ways that should be continued or revived.

Some people in the community may find stressing heritage this way to be inappropriate, arguing that the heritage of the past also included discriminatory patterns of treatment of Native Americans, migrant farm workers, women, or others who were different in any way from the mainstream. This part of heritage, they argue, should not be celebrated as worthy of emulation. The choice of a heritage theme for the festival is thus not a simple issue on which all can agree; it has a political aspect, shaping not only the community's self-presentation to the outside world but also defining a particular stance toward the past and the present. The festival that emphasizes heritage thus creates an "official" memory of the past for the town.

Because small-town festivals efface time, they are well suited to taking on a central role in the memory culture of the people they touch. Because they change little, because they seem to celebrate the community itself, they allow people both to reflect on the past and to create memories that are of the past and that become the past. That is, a small-town festival can become a kind of past in the present; many festivals change so little that, once they begin, it might still seem to be, say, 1975. Yet, there is a danger in the insularity of the festival. It is not 1975 any more, nor 1875. How will the town's heritage help it deal with the challenges that face communities in the 1990s? The question is not an idle one. It may be possible that reflection on a community's heritage has some value for the present in the recognition that the early days were tough, too. On the other hand, the current heritage vogue may also foster a treacherous nostalgia, a longing for a past that never existed—a past of quaint clothing and tools, of charming songs in foreign languages, of children who said "Yes, ma'am" and "No, sir," where pain, dirt, suffering, intensely hard work, dishonesty, and discrimination never existed. Such nostalgia provides reassurance that things are not so bad, if only we can recapture the past. Indeed, nostalgia inhibits change because it directs people's gaze away from their contemporary situation toward the golden light of a stable past that exists only in the fragile and frequently deceptive memories of these same people.

But culture requires both memory and forgetting. The festival conveniently provides both as it creates a play world, neither past nor present, but like any play world, one that exists in its own time. It provides its own architecture, its own social structure and emotional tone, and its own culturally constructed history. In its apparent immutability, the festival world makes possible the performance of community and the creation of the sets of things remembered and things forgotten that create the community symbolically and physically.

Festivals provide people with opportunities to come home, to participate in communitywide traditions, and to experience or reexperience time and space in ways that encourage the building of memories. Festivals have been part of Minnesota life for a long time. Where did they come from? How did the festival model develop?

Summer Fest, Deerwood.

Sinclair Lewis Days, Sauk Centre.

Volunteer fire departments' water-ball fight. Corn Fest, Ortonville.

Water show. Corn Fest, Ortonville.

Kolacky Days, Montgomery.

Demonstration by St. Paul Czech Dancers. Kolacky Days, Montgomery.

Examining old Kolacky Days photographs and newspaper clippings. Kolacky Days, Montgomery.

Pola-Czesky Days, Silver Lake.

Judges interviewing queen candidate in city council meeting room. Kolacky Days, Montgomery.

Onstage during queen pageant: plaque with previous winners' names, oil portrait of reigning queen, tiaras and bouquets for new royalty. Kolacky Days, Montgomery.

Corn Carnival, Cokato.

Evening-gown competition at queen pageant. Sinclair Lewis Days, Sauk Centre.

Presentation of candidates at queen pageant. Corn Carnival, Cokato.

Sinclair Lewis Days, Sauk Centre.

New queen with parents immediately after coronation. Kolacky Days, Montgomery.

After the pageant. Kolacky Days, Montgomery.

Parade. Kolacky Days, Montgomery.

Parade. Watercade, Litchfield.

Turtle race. Corn Fest, Ortonville.

Clown parade. Summer Fest, Deerwood.

Santa Claus makes a parade appearance. Sinclair Lewis Days. Sauk Centre.

Parade. Watercade, Litchfield.

Watercade, Litchfield.

Line for free corn. Cornfest, Ortonville.

2. A TALE OF THREE CITIES

How did community festivals in Minnesota get started? It is a difficult question to answer. The general answer—that human beings are gregarious animals, and festivals bring people together—does not really get to the heart of the question about particular festivals with particular events in particular places. Festivals do develop social solidarity, but some towns that do not have festivals seem to have just as much social solidarity as those that do.

Sometimes people suggest to me that festivals must be connected with the ethnic heritage of the town's residents; that is, residents brought their festival with them from the Old Country. However, few towns have always been dominated by one ethnic group, there is little evidence of traditional Old Country or ethnic festivals in small towns, and today's community festivals are neither very old nor very ethnic.

In 1986, I sent out a questionnaire to 150 communities, asking about (among other things) the origins of their festivals. I received responses from 52 representatives of festivals. Nine respondents did not know when their festival had begun, but of those who did, the responses were as follows:

Prior to 1910	4	9.3%
1920s	2	4.6%
1930s	2	4.6%
1940s	3	7.0%

1950s	3	7.0%
1960s	6	14.0%
1970s	9	20.9%
1980s	14	32.6%
TOTAL	43	100.0%

Only eight of the festivals in the sample, fewer than 20 percent, were started before 1940. About a third of the festivals began in the 1980s. Over 50 percent of the festivals began after 1970. Nearly 12 percent of the festivals were first held in 1976, since the United States Bicentennial provided an opportunity for many civic organizations to consider ways of celebrating. What better way than a festival?

The basis for modern Minnesota community festivals is probably a merging of the Independence Day celebration with the older harvest festival traditions that go back to Europe. The Independence Day tradition goes back to the earliest days of the United States, and Minnesota cities and towns have been celebrating the Fourth of July for many years. Indeed, the particular events that make up the community festival are quite similar to those of the Independence Day celebration. In my survey, six festivals were Fourth of July festivals, and another two had begun as Fourth of July festivals (there were forty-five answers to this particular question).

Kolacky Days in Montgomery

Consider the following report, taken from the *Montgomery Messenger* of June 23, 1916:

Committees are still figuring, planning, and working over time so as to get every detail, down to the finest point, and when the roar of the cannon at dawn shatters the solemn silence of night on July 4th, they will feel satisfied that their labors have not been in vain.

It will be a great event—the biggest, the grandest, the most elaborate affair of its kind attempted here or elsewhere in the county. Approximately $1000.00 will be spent for no other purpose than to entertain the vast throng expected in Montgomery on that glorious day. Three bands will render music: the Montgomery national, the Le Sueur County national, and the Le Sueur center concert band. A baseball game for a purse of $100.00 will be contested at the ball park. Atty. John Lebens of this city will give the address of welcome and John J. Fahey, an eloquent and brilliant attorney of Norwood, Minnesota, will deliver the oration of the day. A grand parade will take place at ten o'clock in which all merchants and manufacturers will participate; forty dollars will be given in cash prizes for this purpose. In the after-noon, following the baseball game, races and sports will take place, for which cash prizes will be awarded, amounting to $150.00. The committee purchased a $90.00 full blood registered Red Poled [sic] bull from Josh Sladek of Greenleaf Lake which will be one year old next July third. Somebody is going to get the animal without cost, merely by registering their name on July 4th while in town. Your name may be the lucky one and you may win the handsome, valuable prize. The drawing will take place at 8:00 in the evening. Hon. John Spence will be the Marshall of the day.

In the afternoon and evening, patriotic music will be rendered on the street, at the baseball field, and at the bowery, where a dancing platform will be erected, especially for this glorious occasion. Meals will be served by the ladies of the Catholic and German Lutheran Churches. In the evening, a grand display of fireworks. When you think of July 4th, think of Montgomery, Minn.

The races and sports included a young men's footrace, young ladies' footrace, fat men's running race, married ladies' footrace, boys' egg race, ladies' ball-throwing contest, pipe race, farmers' footrace, boys' sack race, three-legged race, greased-pig contest, and greased-pole contest.

The festival apparently exceeded the planners' expectations. The *Montgomery Messenger* of July 7, 1916, carried an extensive report on page one under the headline, "Celebration Was Best Ever." The *Messenger* estimated that over six thousand visitors were in town for the festival, nearly five times the city's population. All the downtown businesses were decorated with the flag and red, white, and blue bunting, and more bunting was stretched across Main Street. The official events began ("almost on schedule time") with the parade, "the grandest spectacular and without doubt the longest parade that has ever traversed the streets of this city, or any other city of like size in the state." The parade stretched for twelve blocks and included the fire department and all its equipment, horse-drawn and automobile floats entered by the businesses of the town, decorated automobiles, clowns, comedians, and brass bands from Montgomery, Le Center, and New Prague. Le Center sent a delegation of some seventy-five automobiles carrying what the paper called "practically all the boosters of that town and many farmers residing in its trade territory." Apparently, the large crowd lining the streets for the parade was a demonstrative one, as the *Messenger* reported that there were vociferous cheers and enthusiastic hand clapping for many of the displays.

After the parade, the brass bands began to play at various places about town. At two o'clock, the Montgomery band set up and played for dancing until early the next morning. The baseball game between Montgomery and Le Sueur was a disappointment because, after the second inning, the outcome was never in doubt—Montgomery won 12–6—and the game was not an interesting one. But the races and other downtown activities revitalized the crowd, and the greased-pig and greased-pole contests were particular delights. The vast crowd, according to the report, not only enjoyed the events but also enjoyed itself. "Each individual was interested in looking at the crowd and sizing it up. As we say this feature of the gathering is by far the most transcendently interesting of anything that may be devised. Whenever it comes into play the people have a good time and everybody is satisfied." By evening, the picnic grounds and dancing pavilion were jammed with people who celebrated long into the next morning.

The dinners and suppers served by the ladies of the Catholic and Lutheran churches were apparently popular and reasonably priced. The Alba Hotel was also a popular place for festivalgoers to dine, and lunch counters set up along the streets and at the baseball field provided more casual alternatives. The elated editor summed up the celebration.

> In conclusion we will say that the celebration here last Tuesday was the biggest, the greatest and the most elaborate event of its kind ever attempted here or anywhere else in the county. This is what the Messenger said it would be and we feel confident that we did not exaggerate in the least. The citizens of Montgomery have just reason to feel proud for the creditable manner in which every detail of the program was carried out, and for the good clean amusements furnished to the largest number of visitors that ever assembled at one time in our midst. The citizens of Montgomery contributed liberally to the fund, which made possible the celebration and we believe that every dollar which they donated was well expended—as the advertising which has been and will be derived from such a rousing celebration is inestimable and as years roll by, will be referred to as the most successful Fourth of July ever observed in Montgomery.

In this July 4th of three-quarters of a century ago, there are some clear prefigurations not only of Montgomery's future Kolacky Days but of the modern community festival prototype. Committees organized the 1916 festival in Montgomery, and local businesspeople actively participated in it. It featured many events still popular in festivals today and several different kinds of meals. Overall, the celebration was designed to attract people into town for the festival in hopes that they would continue to patronize Montgomery businesses for all their other needs. In this regard, two items should be noted. First, the grand prize in the drawing was a full-blooded, registered bull calf. This was hardly a prize to attract a city resident. Rather, it was a way to attract farmers into town for the celebration. Indeed, there were forty-five hundred entries in the drawing, and the bull was won by a six-year-old girl who lived with her parents on a farm in Montgomery Township.

Second, the newspaper editor saw clearly the commercial implications of the festival for attracting people to shop and transact their business in Montgomery.

By 1921, a grand-opening dance, held at the White Front Casino, had been added. By the time the first Kolacky Days was held in 1929, the basic model for what goes into a festival was already in place. Blanche Zellmer, Carol Fried, and Susan Augst, in their history of the town, *Montgomery: From the "Big Woods" to the Kolacky Capital, 1856–1976*, write that the idea for the festival came originally from Carl Fischer, special events chairman of the Montgomery Community Club, in September 1929. He proposed a field day in the fall, after the harvest and the vegetable packing at the Green Giant cannery were over. The program was to include, among other things, a "free feed," band concerts, and running races of various kinds. The name Kolacky Days was suggested a week later by the Irish American editor of the *Montgomery Messenger*, John Keohne. The first festival, celebrated on a Tuesday later in the autumn of that year, featured six bands and reportedly attracted six thousand people. A year later, a parade, said to be over one mile long, was added. A year after that, the first queen contest, to find the "Kolacky Kween," was added, and by 1933, it was claimed that thirty thousand attended the festival.

During World War II, Kolacky Days, like most festivals, was not celebrated. In 1948, as life returned to normal, the festival resumed. By the early 1950s, it had moved from late September to late July and had assumed the form it would follow for the next quarter century. The 1950s and 1960s were times of enormous parades featuring state politicians and office seekers, bands, antique cars, trucks, floats, visiting community queens, and more. By the 1970s, however, drinking alcohol in the downtown area, and the behaviors associated with it, had become more than many people in Montgomery were willing to tolerate. In 1980, the Community Club, which was still the civic organization responsible for the festival, moved the major festival events and activities to the largest city park in a successful attempt to separate the bar crowds from the festivalgoers. In the late 1980s, a series of carefully considered moves, including requiring a button for entrance to two of the dances in the park, put Kolacky Days on a solid financial footing.

The Ortonville Corn Festival

Ortonville, the seat of Big Stone County, is located on Big Stone Lake, on the South Dakota–Minnesota border. It, too, had a July 4th celebration that predated the Corn Festival. In 1925, for example, the July 4th festivities included a grand industrial parade, a water sports program, dinner at noon, a formal guard mount by Company L, 135th Infantry, a baseball game, street sports, boat races, a band concert, and fireworks. In its issue of July 9, 1925, the *Ortonville Independent* estimated that a crowd of between five thousand and ten thousand had attended the celebration. At the time, the population of the city of Ortonville was only about fourteen hundred people. The reporter observed that

> the industrial parade was not as large as others staged here, yet most all of the floats were carefully decorated. First prize of $35 went to the Pioneer Store Cooperative Co., which entered a coach automobile elaborately decorated with crepe paper by John Ljungdahl and displaying Munsing Wear advertising. . . . third prize of $15 went to the Tracy-Herzog Produce Co., which entered a float with a profile of the "Father of our Country" in which pullets formed the body.

Here again, much of the crowd came from the surrounding rural areas and from other small towns near Ortonville.

Five years later, following the establishment in town of a corn canning factory, the first festival, then called the Sweet Corn Festival, was celebrated in late August. The factory management, in a public relations gesture, donated enough corn on the cob to provide as much as everyone wanted. The bakery in town agreed to furnish bread, and the local creamery supplied butter.

By 1935, Ortonville was expecting fifteen thousand visitors from a 100-mile radius. The festival's organizers anticipated that this would be the largest crowd in the festival's history and had notices put in the newspaper urging Ortonville residents to volunteer to help serve the corn dinner. There were vaudeville acts, a free program of music from three brass bands, and speeches by prominent speakers. The "pavement dance" that evening featured Amsden's Amblers with dance caller Jim Shannon. There was also a corn-eating contest, claimed to be the world championship, which featured "Korn King" Ed Kottwitz, who had won the corn-eating contest several years in a row. Unlike the earlier July 4th celebrations, the Sweet Corn Festival did not include a parade in its early years. Unfortunately, it rained on August 29, 1935, and the crowd was diminished. Nevertheless, the *Ortonville Independent* claimed that ten thousand people had attended, that free corn dinners had been served to seven thousand, and that Ed Kottwitz had retained his title.

The festival was organized by the Town and Farm Club. The significance of the name should not be missed. It was explicitly designed to bridge the gap between those who lived in town and those on the surrounding farms. By the time I began studying festivals in the late 1970s, this gap had widened into a difficult-to-bridge gulf in many parts of Minnesota. But in the earlier days, the relations between town and country were rather more symmetrical. As late as 1949, Farmers Day was celebrated in Ortonville. This event, which featured a parade, thrill show, ball game, and fireworks, took the place of the Sweet Corn Festival that year. The latter festival was postponed because "of the many observances in this area of the 100th anniversary of the formation of Minnesota Territory." Farmers Day was quite plainly a way of connecting the city with its rural residents, on whom the city was dependent.

By 1955, reference to farmers was not as prominent. Under the August 11 headline, "Throng Expected Here for Annual Sweet Corn Festival," the newspaper editor wrote that the festival that year would feature

> all [the corn] you can eat . . . served with bread and butter, coffee or nectar, at Ortonville's city park, a natural amphitheater, where friend meets friend, neighbor meets neighbor in a good old-fashioned get-together as a climax to the season's bounteous harvest. In deep appreciation for all the patronage you have given them, Ortonville merchants wish to treat you that day.

While the harvest theme was still prominent, the slogan was now "where friend meets friend, neighbor meets neighbor."

This movement away from emphasizing the farm connection and toward stressing the community nature of the festival was not unique to Ortonville, and it corresponded to demographic changes in rural areas and small towns following World War II. The increasing mechanization of agriculture led to fewer people living on the farm. Highway improvements made for easier travel to regional centers for work, shopping, and entertainment. The penetration of local economies by large regional or national entities such as banks, insurance companies, state and federal agencies, restaurant chains, chain stores, and food processing and manufacturing plants decreased the dependence of farmers and small-town residents on each other. An increase in the number of children who had to leave town to find work lessened the solidity of the ties holding the community together.

The Glenwood Waterama

The Glenwood Waterama, too, began as a Fourth of July celebration. The Glenwood Independence Day festivities of 1935 bear a certain resemblance to the mix of events that came to make up Waterama, which began twenty years later. The Glenwood post of the American Legion organized the 1935 celebration, which featured horse races, a baseball game, a sports program, an industrial parade, daylight and night fireworks, dancing at the Lakeside Pavilion, and a raffle with a grand prize of a Ford V-8 car. In the 1980s, the baseball games, sports program, parade, fireworks, dancing, and raffle were still part of Waterama.

In the summer of 1955, James Kinney, the new owner of the local newspaper, the *Pope County Tribune*, arrived in Glenwood from Benson. He was surprised to find that townspeople were not taking advantage of the city's charm and stunning setting on its greatest natural resource, Lake Minnewaska, the thirteenth largest lake in Minnesota. Instead, Glenwood was the site of one of many local July 4th celebrations, and was not attracting many people. In a series of editorials, Kinney proposed that the Independence Day festivities be replaced with a lake-oriented festival on another summer weekend that would attract tourists. He thought it would be a natural draw. By the late fall of that year, the Glenwood Jaycees and Chamber of Commerce had agreed to organize a festival. A contest was held to select a name, and Waterama won.

Kinney was right about the attractiveness of a water festival. The first Waterama was held from August 10 to 12, 1956, and was judged a great success. A traveling carnival was in town for the event, and the first button dance was held at the Lakeside Ballroom on Friday night. Saturday featured a golf tournament, a kiddie parade, a logrolling thrills-and-spills show on the lake, swimming and boat races, and an evening water-ski show followed by a lighted pontoon-boat parade. Sunday began with an amateur water-skiing contest, more golf, a one-hundred-unit parade with eight drum-and-bugle corps, repeats of the water-ski show and logrolling show, the coronation of the Waterama queen, and a gigantic fireworks display. The festival attracted the attention of Minneapolis-based WCCO, one of the dominant radio and television stations in the state. That year, there were two news items from Glenwood on the WCCO television news. And for many years thereafter, WCCO radio personalities were masters of ceremonies for the queen pageant. The newspaper estimated attendance at fifteen thousand, making it the largest celebration that had ever been held in Glenwood. The lighted pontoon-boat parade along the lakefront at night was a highlight of Waterama, and has been ever since. It is the only such parade in Minnesota, perhaps in the entire country.

In 1957, the following year, five thousand buttons were made, to be sold at one dollar each for adults and fifty cents for children. Since button sales were meant to raise funds for the festival's expenses, there were plans to sell buttons door to door, and more events than just the dance required buttons for admission. Governor Orville L. Freeman and Miss Minnesota rode in the parade and attended the queen's luncheon. The button dance featured the well-known band leader Stan Kenton and his dance band.

By 1958, Waterama appeared to be a major Minnesota attraction, claiming to attract thirty-five thousand spectators to the parade, and visitors from all over Minnesota and surrounding states. In the 1960s, the pontoon-boat parade alone reportedly had ten thousand in attendance. Such crowd estimates should be taken with a grain of salt, however, for they are based on guesses and wishful thinking. My students and I have frequently counted the number of those attending an event, and the result has always been much lower than the estimate provided by the organizers or cited in the newspapers. In 1985, for example, twenty-one hundred watched Waterama's lighted pontoon parade, an immense crowd, although much below the estimates made for prior years. During its first twenty years, the standard crowd estimate for Glenwood's street parade was thirty-five thousand. Since the parade route is about fifteen blocks long, that figure would mean nearly twelve hundred people per side of each block, including residential blocks, a crowd of extraordinary density. In fact, in 1985, two of my students counted nearly fourteen thousand people at the Waterama parade, which is one of the largest parade crowds in my research experience.

Waterama has always maintained a focus on Lake Minnewaska. From the beginning, it featured water-ski shows, swimming and amateur water-skiing contests, and sailboat, canoe, or hydroplane races. Perhaps the most unusual use of the waterfront began in 1965, when the Reverend L. D. Kramer organized the nondenominational Lakeside Galilean Service on Waterama Sunday morning. Kramer operated a nursing home in Glenwood and, as a television preacher, was host of *Challenge of Truth,* which ran nationally in the late 1960s and through the 1970s. He was founder and president of what began as the Assembly Homes, based in Glenwood, and later became known as Challenge Ministries, and finally became L. D. Kramer Worldwide Ministries. From the Assembly Homes pontoon float moored at the city park, Kramer preached to increasingly large crowds. By 1968, it was estimated that three thousand people attended the service, and that number stayed relatively constant from year to year. The final Galilean service was in 1979.

Over twenty-five hundred buttons were sold in 1957, and the total expenditures exceeded $5,500. However, total income exceeded expenses by only $25. The financing of Waterama continued to be a problem. Businesses in the late 1950s were contributing a total of $1,500 every year to keep Waterama afloat.

A radical solution to the perennial fund-raising problem was proposed in August 1960, when Admiral Bob Begum, the overall director of Waterama for 1961, suggested raffling off a car at the end of the 1961 queen pageant. The thinking was that with a tremendous effort by the Glenwood Traveling Men's Club to sell tickets outside the area, and a similar effort in town, $10,000 worth of tickets could be sold. After subtracting the cost of the car, there would still be enough money to fund the festival fully. The plan worked, although the original revenue prediction was a bit high. In 1961, $6,088 was raised through button sales, nearly two and one-half times higher than in previous years. This successful strategy continued for more than fifteen years, and the number of buttons sold every year rose steadily. The Waterama organizers were zealous in selling buttons along the parade route. After a couple of years, people were attracted to Glenwood not only by a fine parade (in 1968, before school consolidations and budget cuts, there were thirty marching bands and drum-and-bugle corps) but also by the chance to win a car. The last car raffle was held in 1979. By then, car prices had gotten so high that the raffle would not have made enough money to contribute significantly to the $34,000 budget, even though button sales of over $12,000 had been recorded. By 1980, the top raffle prize was a check for $1,000, and the total cash prizes were worth $4,000.

The budget problems of Waterama, like those of most festivals, were persistent. Although usually finishing in the black, a rainy year or a one-time capital expenditure could leave the festival owing money. Waterama never built up much of a cash reserve until the mid-1980s, when a near disaster had a large payoff. The major threat to any festival, especially one that depends on financing from button sales on the day of the parade, is the weather. A rainy day or two can cut income by more than half. The Waterama organizers, during the festival's third year, had done some archival research and discovered that the weekend which received the least rain over the years was the last full weekend in July. Waterama was immediately switched to that weekend. But there had been scares throughout the succeeding years, even on what was historically the summer's driest weekend. For further protection, the Waterama board began buying a rain insurance policy for the parade, written so that if a specified amount of rain had fallen by noon on the Sunday of the parade, the festival would collect on the policy. A torrential rain hit Glenwood on the parade morning in 1982. The insurance rainfall limit was reached, and the policy came into force. At twelve-thirty, the rain stopped completely, the sun came out, the city dried off, and the parade went off as scheduled with a huge crowd. This provided the cushion that Waterama organizers had been seeking for years. Most festivals are not so fortunate.

Waterama's biggest challenge was a controversy over alcohol consumption on public property, particularly at the Chalet, a campground owned and operated by the city. Like Kolacky Days at about the same time, Waterama was growing and so were its problems. By the mid-1970s, the Chalet campground had become the center for college-age reunions. Students from Glenwood, the nearby University of Minnesota Morris, and other universities would converge on the campground together with significant numbers of beer kegs. In 1979, the *Pope County Tribune* estimated that more than one thousand young people had packed into an area with campsites to accommodate 150 campers. The crowd burned several picnic tables for fuel, overwhelmed the portable sanitary facilities to such a degree that the camping areas were used for excretion, and produced so much garbage that it took three days to clean up the area. Most of the time, the party was confined to the campground, but stories circulated of incidents during the parade each year when drunken men would emerge from the campground to rush the queen floats and pull the queens off. Sometimes, they would also "moon" the crowd. In 1975, police issued 130 tickets during Waterama, a number that continued to rise, reaching 180 tickets in 1979. Countywide, an ordinary summer weekend with a dance or a celebration somewhere in Pope County produced 20 to 25 tickets.

After the 1979 debacle, a battle over Waterama erupted in Glenwood. One group of residents wanted to close the campground and ban the consumption of alcoholic beverages in public places. They argued that conditions were unsafe and unhygienic at the campground, that there was too much disorder, and that the rowdiness offended and disturbed people living near the campground. Further, they contended, the antics of a few drunks were disrupting a family-oriented event, the risk of alcohol-related traffic fatalities had reached unacceptable levels, and the image that this revelry gave Glenwood was not what anyone in town wanted or needed. Another group opposed both proposals, arguing that alcohol use was moderate except at the campground, that the rowdy crowd mostly stayed at the campground, and that for only three days a year a certain amount of festival disorder could be tolerated. The opposing group also countered that the ban on alcohol and the closed campground would kill Waterama, that people who arrived ready to party and found the campground closed would riot, and that it was better to attract people to Glenwood, even if it was to a raucous party at a jammed campground, than to turn them away. The argument led to some surprising rifts in the community, as friends and business associates found themselves on opposing sides.

The issue came to a head at a city council meeting as arguments pro and con were presented. The city council voted to implement the alcohol ban and to close the campground during the festival. The results were gratifying in the extreme. Only 78 tickets were written by the Glenwood police and the Pope County Sheriff's Department. Several visitors, according to a newspaper interview with the police chief, stopped to tell him that they had enjoyed the most pleasant Waterama in years. The county sheriff was quoted in the *Pope County Tribune* of July 31, 1980, as saying, "This was the nicest Waterama to work I can remember. It was quieter for our department than some other week ends." No infuriated would-be campers rioted, and the entire city cleanup was finished by eleven o'clock on Monday morning.

The only problems were that button sales were down and local interest seemed to be waning. Also, there was a seven hundred dollar deficit facing the 1981 organizers; however, the deficit was wiped out in 1981 with button sales that topped fifteen thousand dollars and a huge crowd for all three days of the festival. Attendance was up partly because of the weather and partly, it was argued, because the rowdiness of earlier Wateramas was over. Glenwood's Waterama organizers took an approach that was rather different from that taken by the organizers of Kolacky Days in Montgomery, who did not ban alcohol but, instead, simply moved the festival to the park, away from the area of disorder in the downtown area. In Glenwood, the disorder was in the park's campground, and the campground was closed and alcohol banned so the festival could continue in town.

Some Uses of the Festival Past

What the history of all three of these festivals implies, I think, is that, regardless of what the original Minnesota festival might have been, once the transformation from Fourth of July celebration to weekend community festival had begun, the playing field for communities changed. Once a Kolacky Days, a Corn Fest, and a Waterama were formed, they became the baseline for other communities. If the chamber of commerce in another town wanted a customer appreciation summer project, it had models to copy. If Glenwood's businesses were making a lot of money, if its community service organizations were profiting, and if its name was recognized all over the state, then other towns needed to start their own festivals. This is precisely what has happened.

Minnesota small towns seem isolated as one drives between them through endless fields on a two-lane road laid out with a ruler. Yet they are tied into networks formed by economic and political connections, school sports rivalries, school consolidations, the broadcast ranges of local radio stations, countywide newspapers, and attendance at each other's festivals. People in one town know what is going on in other towns. When I visited Melrose in 1983 to do some research on its fourth Independence Day festival, people there told me about festivals they had attended in Glenwood, Sauk Centre, Greenwald, and New Munich. If a town like New Munich could have a festival, they told me, they should certainly have one in Melrose.

So, as festivals spread across the landscape, they form a context, both historical and cultural, within which members of communities decide what the course of their communities ought to be. The past plays an important role in this, as the weight of community traditions comes to bear and as people interpret the meaning of festival activity in their own and neighboring towns. The past as it is remembered and interpreted is used to justify power relations in the community today, whether this means eliminating farm machinery from the parade, officially recognizing the activities of women in organizing the festival, or having the same elite group of people organize the festival year after year because they always have. In the towns I have visited, there are always a couple of people, usually elderly men, who are the historians of the festival. They are the only ones who seem interested in the details of the past, the identity of the original organizers, what events used to make up the festival, why it began. Most of the other people I have met show, at most, a polite interest in the history of the festival. They are concerned with putting it on now, moving it forward, doing as well as last year, finding their successors. They refer to the past to justify the festival and how it is organized, but they rarely reflect on the past. Yet it is the past that has created the raw materials out of which they work.

3. GROWING UP

Festivals are very much a part of the way communities measure time. From kiddie-parade participants to high school marching-band members to queen-pageant contestants to festival organizers to senior royalty, community members may use the public sequence provided by the festival to mark the stages of life.

The Queen Pageant

We can look at the festival's function of marking life's stages both over the course of years and at a single moment in time. The queen pageant provides a useful illustration. In most communities, candidates at the queen pageant are selected from the young women who have just graduated from high school. The candidates think of themselves as having at least one thing in common—their high school class. People in town think of them that way, too. Almost all the candidates have lived their entire lives in the community. They are known to most of the people in the audience. They have marched in kiddie parades and have been classmates, outstanding athletes, and excellent students. They have been employees, the girls next door, the friends' daughters who have now grown up.

Most of them plan to attend college, and a few will go to vocational and technical schools. When they stand onstage together, a period of their lives in the community is over, and the passage of another year is marked for those in attendance. These young women have come of age. About to leave the community for more schooling, they stand before their fellow citizens one last time to acknowledge that they have been shaped by the community. In most towns, the queens (at least) rarely return permanently after they leave. In Glenwood, for example, of the twenty-six queens between 1956 and 1981, only two were living in Glenwood or environs in 1984; eight were living in other states. At the last moment of their residence in town, these young women embody the role of community representatives. In doing so, they present the community with an image that is deeply satisfying, although it is constructed at a certain cost.

A new generation of girls has grown up, and every year the town pauses momentarily in a ritualized form of play to honor that fact. For audience and candidates alike, the queen pageant provides a way of not letting the transformation slip by unnoticed. Important life-cycle rituals provide a measure far more ancient than the rigid movement of the clock and provide us with the opportunity to reflect on the passage of time. The queen pageant is the small-town equivalent of the debutante presentation. The emphasis of the presentation is to reveal to the community the social nature of growing up and the quality of a town that can produce so many lovely, talented young women.

Every year, the local newspaper features photographs and biographies of the candidates on the front page. Through this annual public announcement, even people who will not attend the queen pageant receive the message of the passage of time and the growing up of the community's children. Under the headline "1984 Miss Hinckley Pageant Underway," for example, the *Hinckley News* of June 28, 1984, proclaimed:

> The Korn and Klover Karnival is approaching and the Miss Hinckley Pageant is underway. A number of local young women have been asked to be a part of the pageant.
>
> Various businesses are involved as sponsors making this event possible. Because of their sponsorship, they have the privilege of choosing a candidate to represent their business in the pageant.
>
> One requirement for the pageant is that the candidate be an incoming Senior in Hinckley High School. The reason for this is because the Queen will be representing Hinckley throughout the coming year in several parades in surrounding communities, and she also needs to be available for the coronation next year.
>
> . . . Judging for the pageant will take place on Friday evening, July 13, beginning at 5 p.m. at the Hinckley High School. The candidates will be judged on the following: Appearance, Poise, Personality, Community Interest and Communications.

. . . We are proud of these fine young women who are willing to represent Hinckley and know they will be a good reflection of our community. We wish them all
good luck.

Not all the young people of the community participate in the pageant, of course.
Young men are completely excluded, but so are quite a few young women, usually the majority of the high school class. Some young women who are eligible are
out of town, busy with other obligations, or unwilling or afraid to prepare a talent presentation. Others simply do not wish to participate. But others are not seen
as suitable participants. There are several reasons for this.

Most candidates have been quite active in school-related extracurricular activities. The biography of the 1991 Miss Sauk Centre, Michelle Winter, as published
in the local newspaper and the queen pageant program booklet, reads:

> Shelly is the daughter of Larry and Rosie Winter. She was active in volleyball,
> basketball, and was captain of the football cheerleaders during the winter season.
> Shelly was involved in the One-Act play, Three-Act play, and was voted "best ac-
> tress" by her peers. She was a member of the speech team, prom committee, and
> D.E.C.A. Chapter. She served on the Student Council as President of her class for
> the past two years and was Treasurer and Vice-President when she was a member
> of the Gopher Prairie 4-H Club. Shelly, an honor student, was awarded the Presi-
> dential Academic Award, and was listed in the "Who's Who Among American
> High School Students." Shelly enjoys writing poetry, listening to country-western
> music, being outdoors, and spending time with her family and friends.
>
>   In the fall, Shelly will attend Mankato State University where she plans to study
> International Relations and Foreign Languages.

The style of this biography is typical of queen-candidate biographies from all over
the state. The biography first situates the candidate in the community; she is the
daughter of specific people, and mentioning them is not only a way of honoring
them and recognizing their part in her success, it is also a way of placing her precisely in the social world of the community. It then lists her school and community accomplishments, emphasizing with the past tense that this part of her life is
over. The biography then turns to her present interests, which, we assume, will
continue to be part of her life—poetry, music, the outdoors, family, and friends.
Finally, her future is highlighted. She is going somewhere for further education
and has an idea of what she will become as an adult. The product of her community, she is now ready to begin life as an adult.

Information gathered at twenty community queen pageants suggests that the
ideal candidate is a young woman who is upwardly mobile. In most towns, the
queen and her princesses are awarded scholarship money, a prize that presumes

the candidates will be pursuing some kind of postsecondary education. Thus some possible contestants are eliminated. The queen pageant is, therefore, not for everyone. Nevertheless, it claims universality. The language employed by organizers, candidates, and the official voice of the pageant as seen in the newspapers and heard from the master of ceremonies onstage, however, suggests that the candidates are presented as if they were *all* the young people of the community. It is an image of the community that is flattering to community members. Who would not be proud of such outstanding young women—lovely, talented, smart, serious, sensitive, active—as they all are? For at least a moment, people are invited to believe that these young women are the community of the future. The shock and disappointment, then, are even greater if (as has happened) a reigning queen becomes pregnant and has to give up her position.

The process of selecting a queen and princesses begins long before the pageant. Sauk Centre, located in the central part of the state, is a city of some thirty-eight hundred people. The boyhood home of Sinclair Lewis, the city is still not entirely sure how to commemorate its most famous native son, who so harshly portrayed it in *Main Street.* For the moment, it is his name that draws tourists off Interstate 94 into town, and so the community festival is named after him. A representative of Sinclair Lewis Days visits the high school in April each year to invite the young women of the senior class to consider becoming one of the ten or twelve candidates for Miss Sauk Centre. The representative tells them what is expected of candidates and winners, how much time is involved, and how the pageant and the subsequent responsibilities of the winners are handled. Usually, the committee receives applications from more young women than the pageant can accommodate. The committee holds a meeting for would-be candidates and their parents in May. The organizers discuss the expectations for candidates and their parents, and they emphasize the responsibilities of the eventual queen and her two princesses. At this point, several young women usually reconsider and do not continue. Conflicting schedules, vacations, summer jobs, worry about the talent competition, and loss of interest take their toll. After all, the candidates are busy in May and June, and still busier preceding the coronation itself in July. For the three winners, the schedule then becomes hectic. They must attend all the remaining events of Sinclair Lewis Days and spend many weekends, with at least one parent as chaperone, going to parades and festivals in other towns throughout the state—Greenwald, Glenwood, Long Prairie, Waite Park, Willmar, Osakis, Spicer, and more—before the summer is over. The following summer there are more parades before Sinclair Lewis Days and the crowning of a new queen and princesses, and then, after that, the Minneapolis Aquatennial. Not every family has that kind of time to spare.

Once the field of candidates is the right size, the young women find themselves entering a whirl of activities unlike anything they have previously experienced. In early May, each finds a business to sponsor her and collects the $85 sponsorship fee. Each then has her picture taken at the local photographer's studio. These photographs will appear in the bank window, in the local newspaper, and in the queen pageant program booklet. Later in May, working in pairs, the candidates solicit ads for the program book from chamber of commerce members in Sauk Centre. Each candidate has to sell twenty-five Sinclair Lewis Days buttons as well. They also attend two or three pageants in other towns to get some ideas about how these events work. As the pageant approaches, they must be present for radio station interviews, rehearsals, various informal events, and a session on hair and makeup hints, a talk that includes information about poise, confidence, how to handle winning and losing, and more. Some years there is a brunch at city hall on the day of the pageant. Finally, the week arrives. Rehearsals begin in earnest, in the evenings, since most of the candidates work during the day.

I was invited to a rehearsal in Sauk Centre in 1987. As I made my way down the darkened hall at the elementary school, I could hear the sounds of the rehearsal coming from the stairway that leads to the basement auditorium. There were the sounds of hammering and of music playing, and as I walked down the stairs, I began to hear voices. Sitting on the steps, the outgoing royalty were holding practice interviews with each of the candidates. Using the questions that had been asked the previous year, they were coaching the candidates to be outgoing, to speak clearly, and to give long answers. As I listened, I was struck by the difference between the queen and her princesses, just finished with their first year of college, and the candidates, who had just graduated from Sauk Centre High School. The candidates were diffident, hesitant, and spoke softly and briefly. The royalty were self-possessed, outgoing, seasoned college students, and they had been through the routine before. They were encouraging to the candidates, who seemed to appreciate the help.

I moved on toward the music onstage, where one of the candidates was practicing her talent presentation, a gymnastics floor exercise. The stagehands looked on impassively, ready to roll the mats up and take them offstage as quickly as possible when she finished. Setting the stage for each talent presentation takes time, and presentations with many props like the mats take the longest. Fortunately, in Sauk Centre, the companies that help sponsor the pageant are recognized with short advertisements read by the emcees during the times the curtains are closed, and thus the time between talent presentations is filled.

When the gymnast completed her routine, the organizers called all the candidates together. They needed to practice their walk out onto the stage and down the runway again, and to work on turning and waving. Walking, turning, and waving from the stage are not easy; big-time pageant competitors—those at the Miss Minnesota and Miss America contests—achieve effortless grace only by hours of practice. Each candidate was wearing a hoop slip for this part of the rehearsal so that she could have the feeling of walking in a formal gown without having to wear one for practicing. The pageant organizer reminded the candidates to look straight toward the audience or toward the back wall, to remember not to swing their arms as they walked, and to smile ("You're having fun!"). The emcees had just arrived, and they began reading the names and the accomplishments of each candidate. That evening, the candidates were not yet ready for the pageant. They listened intently but continued to do the things the organizer had just told them not to do. Some still walked heavily onto and across the stage and made their turns only after thinking about what came next. Others were still swinging their arms or not standing straight, and most forgot to smile. The pageant organizer shouted at one to stop walking as if she were carrying milking pails to the barn. They ran through it again and again. Each time the candidates did better. They spent well over an hour walking out onto the stage, turning, waving, and walking back. That much practice is not unusual; I have seen it wherever I have attended pageant rehearsals.

The organizers decided to run through the entire pageant in order from beginning to end, omitting only the outgoing royalty's farewell slide show about their experiences together representing Sauk Centre. I watched for a while, noticing that when they were not onstage, the outgoing royalty returned to the stairwell with a candidate to practice interviews. Another hour and a half passed and the talent presentations were still not complete. On my way out, I stopped to talk with the organizer; some of my students and I were going to come back the next day and help them with the stage decoration.

Four years have passed since then, and I am back at Sinclair Lewis Days again. The day of the pageant has been hot. The auditorium is not air conditioned, but it is below ground level, so I am hopeful that it will be cool. For a few moments, it is. Then, at six-thirty, the crowd comes surging in! In what seems like almost no time at all, over eight hundred people are sitting in the auditorium, and it is hot, humid, and quite still. Although dressed for the weather in shorts or summer dresses, the audience is already suffering before the pageant has even begun. Programs are waving all throughout the auditorium as people try to get a little breeze moving. The pageant is supposed to begin at seven, but it is a bit late getting underway. Finally, the lights dim and the music starts. The candidates, in casual matching outfits appear, dancing together in a choreographed production number. The crowd cheers and applauds. The curtain closes, and the emcees, two local businessmen in their late twenties, appear. They are in tuxedos, and they banter with each other for a few moments before they introduce the outgoing queen and her princesses. The three walk out, greeted by thunderous applause, and wave in a coordinated, practiced way. This year they have chosen to perform a little skit together.

Finally, it is time to meet the candidates. The talent presentations come first. Each candidate is announced and the curtain opens. The lights come up on a motorcycle and a young woman in a leather jacket. The accompanist begins, and the candidate sings "Leader of the Pack." She receives polite applause, bows, and exits. The emcees return with a few commercial announcements, and the curtain opens again. Three young men and a queen candidate dressed in Spanish style are onstage. The sound system plays "Spanish Eyes," and the candidate lip-synchs the song and dances with the young men. She receives a rather enthusiastic reception, and is followed by the first humorous skit of the evening, which is about a young girl's first crush.

The next performance is complicated. The candidate performs a skit in which she speaks, plays the theme from the film *Terms of Endearment* on the piano, and shows a series of slides of sunsets, babies, butterflies, waves, sailboats, small animals. This draws tremendous applause from the audience, and even some cheers. The curtains finally close. The emcees now take a long time bantering with each other, telling jokes and reading ads for chamber of commerce businesses that have paid to sponsor the pageant. When the curtains reopen, we all see why the delay was so long. The mats have been laid in place and a candidate in gymnastics attire comes out. She is a good high school gymnast and impresses the crowd, which applauds loudly. The curtain closes and opens again to reveal the piano. We get a good ragtime piano piece from the next candidate.

The next performance is the most remarkable one I have ever seen at a queen pageant. The curtains open partly, revealing two Greek columns that form a doorway. The candidate, who later will be crowned Miss Sauk Centre, appears between the columns in a simple loose costume and performs Medea's soliloquy from Euripides' *Medea*. It is rather a good performance, but the sheer outrageousness of going from the frothy, light presentations that make up the ordinary talent show fare to the dark intensity of Greek tragedy takes the breath away. The audience is stunned, but recognizing that it should salute great art and a strong performance, it gives the candidate strong applause.

It must be difficult for the remaining candidates to follow Euripides. We have a song, "Get Here"; a performance of a movement from Beethoven's Moonlight Sonata; an aerobics routine; a supposedly humorous skit about a young girl taken in by advertising; and, finally, a song from *Les Miserables,* "I Dream the Dream."

The final performance is not bad, but like nearly all the singing I have heard at pageants, the singer's voice is throaty and unsupported.

Many queen pageants have talent competitions, and the performances are usually acceptable if not really very good. Nevertheless, the audiences seem to enjoy and reward these performances with applause, cheers, and praise. However, if we apply professional performance standards or even good student-performance standards to these talent presentations, we cannot help rating much of what we see and hear as mediocre or poor. Hence, we are puzzled by an audience that is so enthusiastic. Have they no taste? No standards? Can they not hear how badly off-key this singer is? How wooden this acting? How poorly phrased this saxophone lick? One of my students wrote of a different pageant:

> I listen to a very amateur performance by [the candidate,] who sings partially off key through her song. Someone beside me says, "She was great, that was excellent!" I can only assume their criteria for judging are different than mine. This group of spectators is an intense support system for the whole group of queen candidates: they could do nothing wrong. . . . Could the attempt at trying to achieve what may be out of reach for any competitor be enough to satisfy the expectations of this community? I can't help but feel that winning is not the goal here, but trying is. Then the high praise for [the candidate's] amateur performance makes sense. I recognize the intense support as similar to what parents and friends would give to children under five for attempting something totally new, without expectations of success. The pride of the spectator is in witnessing growth and development.

The rules for judging *are* different, and in the ways my student suggests. The queen pageant is about accomplishments, growth, and development, not about exceptional performances. Most of us are capable of a talent show performance, but it certainly takes courage and determination to stand up in front of eight hundred neighbors, friends, and strangers, and perform, especially when you are well aware that your presentation does not resemble that of the performers you see on television. This is particularly true in small-town Minnesota. As essayist, novelist, and observer of small-town life, Carol Bly, comments:

> Our style, in the countryside, is not to criticize children at all: we very seldom tell them the plane model was glued carelessly and the sleeve set in without enough easing. (The counterpart of this is that we seldom praise them much for anything either. "You played a real good game against Dawson"; "You did a real good job of that speech contest"—not "I knew you'd do well at the speech thing: I didn't know that I would cry—in fact I'm *still* moved by what you said!") So the children develop neither stamina about criticism nor the imagination to picture to themselves gigantic praise if they excel. They live lightly handed into a middle world of little comment, and therefore little incitement to devotion. . . .

At the same time, Minnesota rural life gives comfort and sweetness. Our young
people are always returning home on their college weekends. When they drop out
of college they tend to wander back here instead of prowling the streets of San
Francisco or St. Paul. Apparently they garner genuine comfort from the old famil-
iarity, the low-intensity social life, and with it a pretty good guarantee of not being
challenged. (Bly 1981, 37,38)

Bly, who is clearly critical but also impassioned and hopeful, is trying to help people rethink their worlds and change them. But her point is important in the context of the queen pageant. In terms of growing up, the queen pageant is not about
being the best or preparing for a professional stage career; it is about fitting in,
doing well, and demonstrating poise, confidence, and capacity. A good analog is
another coming-of-age ceremony in the United States, the Jewish bar mitzvah or
bat mitzvah. At this ceremony, thirteen-year-olds demonstrate their religious coming of age by reading from the Torah, chanting a passage from the Prophets, leading several prayers in front of the congregation—all in Hebrew—and making a
speech relating the week's reading from the Bible to present-day concerns. Yet, no
one expects these young people to sound like cantors and rabbis, who are the
models of chanting and preaching. Anyone expecting to hear magnificent singing
and an intellectually stimulating speech on the great religious and moral questions
of the day will almost certainly be disappointed. But someone expecting to see a
young person taking his or her place in the community through the performance
of a community-defined set of activities that stand for long training and a willing-
ness to accept commitment will be pleased to see that child's growth to adulthood. It does not matter how *well* he or she does it, what matters is that they *do*
it. As the graduate-school joke, designed to relieve the stress of those trying to finish a dissertation, goes: What do they call the person whose accepted dissertation
is the year's worst? The answer: Doctor. So it is with the talent competition.

The candidates are offstage now, changing into their evening gowns, most of
which were senior prom dresses a couple of months earlier. To fill the time, the
emcees introduce the judges, and then follows what to some people is the least interesting part of a queen pageant: the seemingly interminable introduction of the
"visiting royalty." These are the queens and princesses from other towns who
have been invited to ride in the parade and observe the coronation. They validate
the work of the pageant, since they are the community that the home royalty will
join. It is to measure up to, perhaps to surpass, these young women that the local
young women are selected. They will enter, for a while, this world of queens and
princesses who travel about as community representatives.

Nearly one hundred young women in evening gowns step onto the stage, hear their names announced, wave, and walk off. The young people in the audience are not bored, according to my students. The high-school-age females look at the dresses, the hair, and the makeup. The young males in the audience look for interesting and attractive reasons to visit other towns. Overall, the audience can judge how their representatives compare with these queens and princesses from towns both larger and smaller than Sauk Centre.

To map the places where a town's queen and princesses visit would be to draw the rural and urban networks of the state: of neighboring towns, of towns that feel they have some connection with one another, of sports and commercial rivalries, of friendships among organizers. Such a map would also reveal the dominance of Minneapolis and St. Paul. Representatives of the Minneapolis Aquatennial and the St. Paul Winter Carnival regularly attend small-town pageants to drum up business for their festivals, to draw the local royalty to these urban events, and to symbolize the primacy of these two metropolitan areas, home to half the state's people. The urban festivals' representatives are older and appear more sophisticated—successful businessmen in elaborate costumes and uniforms, and women in their mid-twenties in elegant gowns that are clearly not their senior prom dresses.

When all members of the visiting royalty have been introduced, it is time for the evening-gown competition. This part of the pageant has been carefully rehearsed, and the hours pay off. Each candidate seems to glide effortlessly along the stage and the runway, turning at the right spots, waving easily, and smiling, smiling, smiling. As each walks out, her biography is read aloud. After the last has been presented, all the candidates come out together, standing in an arc across the stage. This is a key moment of the pageant: here are the town's young women at the edge of adulthood, begowned and elaborately made-up and coiffed. The audience begins to pay closer attention now, as the judges are excused to make their decision.

The outgoing royalty step onstage to say good-bye. This is an important ritual in every pageant. The young women are expected to become emotional as they pay tribute to the community they represented for the previous year. Each princess and then the queen recounts, often at great length, her royal experiences. She then thanks every friend and relative, weeps, and thanks the other two members of the royalty group, the pageant organizers, and the festival leadership. Some years, the Sauk Centre organizers tape these farewell speeches ahead of time and play them as the queen and princesses take a last walk along the runway. The audience usually gives the outgoing queen a standing ovation, and this year is no exception.

It is time for decisions to be announced. The level of expectation in the auditorium goes up. One can see that the candidates are nervous. They are still smiling, but the smiles are a little tense. The head judge hands the envelopes to one of the emcees. The winner of the talent competition is announced first, applauded, and given a trophy. The evening-gown winner is announced second, and is given a gift. There is applause, but it is edgy, and not overwhelming. We are too close to the real decisions now for the audience to get much involved in celebrating these minor awards. Miss Congeniality is the third award to be announced. Earlier in the day, the young women themselves voted for the candidate who was most fun, most pleasant, most supportive. The new Miss Congeniality receives a plaque.

At last comes the moment that transforms the queen pageant from a showcase for the outstanding young women of the community to a competition with winners and losers. The candidates link hands. The emcees call over the outgoing second princess, open the envelope, and show her the name of her replacement. Tiara in hand, she walks to the candidates, initiating what becomes at some pageants moments of sadistic torture. The outgoing princess, or more often the queen, sometimes walks back and forth slowly, pausing occasionally, nearly putting the crown on one candidate's head only to snatch it away at the last second. After repeating this ritual two or three times, the agony finally ends with a sudden descent of the crown, revealing the winner. In Sauk Centre, however, things are less stressful. The second princess reaches the far side of the arc of candidates, the emcee announces the winner's name, and the second princess places the tiara on the winner's head and hugs her warmly. The candidates on either side also embrace the winner, and she is led to the center of the arc, where three chairs are set out. Handed a bouquet of flowers, she sits.

It is the turn of the first princess. The same procedure is repeated, and now only ten candidates stand onstage. At last, the queen comes forward with the crown to find out the name of her replacement. She walks out in front of the candidates and back toward the middle of the line of candidates. The master of ceremonies speaks: "Ladies and Gentlemen, your 1991 Miss Sauk Centre . . . Michelle Winter!" The crown comes down, Michelle's eyes widen, and her hands jump to her mouth. The crowd cheers and all the other candidates and outgoing royalty engulf her. Tearfully, she adjusts her crown, receives the ribbon proclaiming her to be Miss Sauk Centre 1991, and takes the bouquet of red roses handed to her. Clearly moved, she walks out onto the runway to acknowledge the cheers of the audience. As the applause dies down and the pageant ends, the fathers of the candidates come onstage to escort them down the stairs at the end of the runway and down the main aisle of the auditorium to a reception held in honor of all the candidates. The new princesses and the queen, on the arms of their proud fathers, are the last to sweep up the aisle, and the crowd, released from the sweltering auditorium, surges out.

It has rained during the two and one-half hours we were inside, and the air has cooled. Many members of the audience stop briefly to congratulate the pageant participants in the cafeteria, where cookies and punch are being served. Young women near the candidates' age rush up to the new queen and embrace her, shrieking with excitement. The queen and the princesses are already beginning to separate from the other candidates. All eyes are on them now; they have been chosen. The crowd has thinned out, and most of the unsuccessful candidates and their families have gone home through the wet streets. For the three winners, still being photographed and interviewed, the summer has taken a new direction.

The queen pageant plays an interesting and sometimes important role in the development of the young women who participate in it—a role that lies at the heart of the feminist critique of such events. Reproducing social relations from one generation to the next generation is a challenge that members of any social system face. There is always conflict in this process, as different pressures and interests influence how social roles, attitudes, values, and status are passed on. The queen pageant is one of the ways that a particular vision of what it means to be a woman can be transmitted. The first and most obvious way is the absence of anything for young men that is analogous to the pageant. The experiences of growing up female and of growing up male in a small community with a queen pageant, then, are different in terms of the public display of gender. Adolescent males play sports, play in the marching band, and act in school plays. Adolescent females also participate in those activities, but those who take part in queen pageants learn a unique lesson about the ways appearance and luck are significant determinants of success for women as they move into the adult world.

Organizers and participants strenuously argue that the queen pageant is not a beauty pageant. Still, it is not hard for candidates and spectators alike to get the idea that a young woman's appearance is the key to her success in the pageant. It seems similar to events like the Miss America competition, and many candidates, when interviewed after the pageant, are of the opinion that appearance mattered more than they had thought it would. For many of them, this may well be the first time that their appearance has been so obviously and officially central to their success or failure. Most candidates have been active in school sports, where looks are irrelevant and what counts is performance. But in the queen pageant, they present themselves to the community onstage and silent, heavily made-up, in evening gowns, and with their hair carefully styled. In a few queen pageants, they wear swimsuits and high-heel pumps. The judges, who are almost never local residents, can only judge on the basis of what they see and what they hear in the twenty-minute personal, private interview. As one judge remarked in 1984, "Look, we want someone who will look good waving from a float."

Luck also appears to become a legitimate criterion for success. While the candidates are usually told that the interview is worth 50 percent, the evening gown 12.5 percent, the talent competition 12.5 percent, and poise and oral introduction 25 percent, they are not always sure how the judges interpret those criteria or, indeed, whether those are even the real criteria. Here again, the contrast with athletics is revealing. The criteria for success in sports are dramatically clear—make the baskets, run faster, throw the shot farther—as are the steps to accomplish them—practice, practice, practice. When young women participate in a queen pageant, personal engagement and control over outcomes diminish. Based on our interviews with candidates, we learned that they ask themselves questions like: What do the judges want to hear? How much should I push? What effect will this talent presentation have? How do I look in this dress? Does anything I do have any effect at all? This uncertainty is heightened by the procedure frequently employed at the moment of coronation, when each outgoing princess and queen physically crowns her successor after a long and tantalizing performance of "indecision." Finally, the winner is selected. The result of the teasing is a heightening of the sense that the winner is almost accidental. Any of the young women could have won, there is no certainty, and the judges' decision seems to have been even more mysterious and unpredictable than first thought. As the queen passes with the crown, each candidate still has a chance. Perhaps it will be she who is the lucky one, a phrase sometimes used by the master of ceremonies. Because the judges' decision is frequently not the popular choice, luck becomes increasingly important to the perceptions of candidates and audience alike.

My point here is that, while there are a multitude of influences on women and men of all ages regarding issues of gender, the queen pageant is one of the public events in which gender differences are performed, highlighted, and taught. But because the queen pageant is play, candidates and audience alike have the opportunity to discount the "official" message of the pageant, and some do. Some potential candidates refuse to participate because they find the queen pageant offensive; others who participate may later reject the messages about gender as their experiences take them in other directions. For many candidates, however, the queen pageant is yet another site at which the conventional gender roles of one generation are strengthened and made to seem an inevitable part of growing up female.

Festivals Elsewhere in the Life Cycle

Although the queen pageant probably marks the passage of time most dramatically, it is not the only festival event to do so. The kiddie parade provides a way to introduce the children of the community to the community. Children, usually wearing Halloween costumes or costumes depicting fairy-tale or television characters, march in groups according to the characters they represent. In the past few years, these have included Peter Pan, Wendy, John, and Michael; Little Bo Peep and her sheep; Teenage Mutant Ninja Turtles; Ghostbusters; soldiers; princesses; the Flintstones; North Stars, Vikings, and Twins players; clowns; flowers; ballerinas; and many more. The children fill the streets, some puzzled, others fearful, others proud, most satisfied to be there. Towns organize the kiddie parade in different ways. The kiddie parade may precede the main parade by a few minutes, or follow the same route at a different time or on a different day, or take place in a separate location. In all cases, however, the audience consists of more than doting parents and grandparents. Those along the kiddie parade route admire the costumes, exclaim over the charm of the children, and try to figure out the kinship relationships of the children in the parade to other people in the community. And indeed, the children, the costumes, and the little scenes are adorable, and the children's various expressions and performances are instantly recognizable to any parent. If our children are our future, then the kiddie parade, like the queen pageant, provides one view of that future, affirming that it will be in good hands.

Still, not everyone likes kiddie parades, and some festivals do not have one. "It's not for the kids," they say. "They don't make the costumes. It's a way for the moms to compete, to show off." At times, this seems to be true. Some costumes are wonderfully elaborate, and occasionally one can see parents pushing the children along to compete in the parade, in the same way that parents may push "suitable" girls into the queen pageant. Once again, we see that festivals can serve as arenas for competition as well as cooperation. Where there is no kiddie parade, festival organizers sometimes explain that they do not want to have the children serving as tokens that parents can use to compete with each other. The kiddie parade, they say, should be for the children and by the children. For this reason, in some towns, any child who wants one is given a sheet of poster board and can make whatever he or she wants with it—a drawing, a costume, a sign—and march with it in the kiddie parade.

However it is done, the children, the future of the town, are revealed at their most innocent and most public. They all seem to be there, playing, imagining, just being children (or what adults imagine children to be), and it is easy to be moved. The economy may be tough, there may be controversy in town, school consolidation may be around the corner, regional shopping malls may be sucking the life out of the business district, but for the moment there the children are, and there seems to be hope.

Other moments in the public life cycle are also played out in festivals. For many adolescents, the high school marching band is an important element of life. A number of communities today support a large high school band with well over one hundred members: banner carriers, flag bearers, honor guard, drum majors, flag twirlers, majorettes, and musicians. Rehearsals are long and marching routines are complex, requiring phenomenal precision. The band members seem to thrive on the challenge, and the parents are delighted, too, since rehearsing and marching in festival parades give their children a constructive and entertaining way to pass the long summer vacation. As one parent said to me (and, no doubt, as many parents have often said), "It keeps them out of trouble." When the hometown band marches by, the cheers and applause are long and loud. The spectators seem to acknowledge that these are their town's children, who have worked hard practicing their instruments and marching, and who have achieved something wonderful.

Indeed, the sight and sound of a good high school marching band are impressive: the deep, almost earthshaking power of the low brass, the rhythmic drive and thunder of the drum line, the sheer volume of sound, the precise marching, the snap of the flags as the flag twirlers go through their routines. The scene is sometimes a little disturbing. The band members all look so serious, so intent on being just like everyone else, so concerned about marching with almost robotic precision, mimicking the rigor of a military parade. But once the parade is over, the band members, released from their uniforms and precision marching, celebrate. For them, the pleasures are in being with others their own age, performing complex activities in a competitive environment, and the thrill of the music and the coordinated group effort. For the local people at the parade, the pleasure is in the sight of their young people at another stage of their lives in the community.

After children graduate from high school, there is a lull in their involvement in festivals. As citizens reach their late twenties and establish families and businesses, they begin to be recruited into the organizing body of the festival. From a festival point of view, this is an indication that they have reached full adult status. Helping to organize the festival is not only a way for businesspeople to achieve visibility in town, to serve the community, and, for newcomers to the town's business community, to signal their commitment to the town; it is also a way of marking full membership in the adult life of the community.

As people age and retire, there are still ways for them to be involved in the festival, symbolically marking this transformation into old age. They have not only retired from their jobs, they also may signal their social transformation by retiring from the organizing body of the festival. They can mark their position in the community by taking part in events exclusively for senior citizens: a "golden-age day" with events that honor older members of the community, bus trips from the senior center to festival events, visits by queen candidates to senior citizens at the Legion hall, events held at retirement or nursing homes or in the senior day center. Finally, some festivals offer a senior royalty contest in association with the town's nursing homes. In some of these pageants, the queen candidates, or the queen and her princesses, select the senior king and queen. In other cases, it is the nursing home residents or senior-center members themselves who choose the winners. Regardless, the contest is a clear maker of participants' position as *elderly* within the community.

Because festivals recur summer after summer, a means of reflecting on the passage of time and marking people's movement through socially recognized moments in time is regularly available to the community. It is, I think, a powerful satisfaction, and one of the ways that festivals build community.

4. BUILDING COMMUNITY

The sun is beginning to set over Lake Minnewaska. The shadows lengthen, the light turns golden, the surface of the lake begins to sparkle. A lone fisherman in his boat on the lake is becoming a silhouette. Along the lakeshore drive, next to the Glenwood park, lights begin to go on around the food stands. They are amber, white, green, and red, and they glimmer weakly in the setting sun. The breeze freshens slightly, ruffling the surface of the lake and mixing the summer smells of lake and park with those of well-heated charcoal grills, hamburgers, bratwurst, tacos, popcorn, and barbecued chicken.

Lots of people are out strolling up and down the drive, now closed to traffic, pausing to greet friends or consider the dining possibilities. The picnic tables in the park, and even the cinder-block-and-board benches in front of the bandstand, are beginning to fill up with people ready to eat. Some carry coolers from home, packed with cold fried chicken, sandwiches, hot dogs, potato salad, lettuce, vegetables, apples, casseroles, pies. Others carry heaping paper plates of chicken hot off the grill, baked beans, coleslaw, and a dinner roll from the Jaycees' chicken barbecue. Some are eating the bratwurst, burgers, tacos, burritos, french fries, fried cheese curds, cotton candy, or ice cream from the food stands along the lakeside. From the nearby band shell, the sounds of the high school band tuning up fade, and there is a smattering of applause as the conductor steps up. The band starts to play, and now the lights in the park come on. The park is glorious at this hour, light and breeze playing on the lake and the giant elms, and the crowd of people so clearly enjoying this evening in July.

As it draws closer to nine o'clock, there is still light in the sky, but there is a stir in the crowd and a direction to its movement. More people are out now, gathering outside the Lakeside Ballroom. As the ballroom's doors open, the sounds of the Erv Reutzel Orchestra's old-time music float out, to be picked up by the breeze for a moment. Tonight is the button dance. To gain entrance, people need to wear the official 1981 Glenwood Waterama Button to show that they support the festival. The crowd grows bigger. It seems as though everyone in town is inside or just outside the ballroom. People have told me all week long that the button dance is the big social event of the year, that everyone, even those who do not attend other Waterama events, shows up. Now I believe them. Inside the ballroom, all the booths are filled with the middle aged and the elderly. Young people are standing on the dance floor and anywhere else they can find. People are dancing, talking, drinking beer or soda pop, greeting people they have not seen all year. Back outside, in the deepening twilight, the Waterama leadership has gathered, three men in white blazers and white western hats. With them are fourteen young women, lovely in evening gowns—the Waterama queen candidates. In a few moments, the candidates will be officially presented for the first time to their community, gathered in the ballroom. A drumroll sounds from inside, the door opens, and the young women and the three men move across the street and into the ballroom. Applause and cheers are heard as each candidate is introduced. The dance continues.

Community Identity

Festival organizers and community residents frequently say that their festivals build community, and frequently they are right. But what do they mean by community, and why do they think it is necessary?

Across Minnesota, summer evenings similar to that in Glenwood are part of community building through festivals. Townspeople eat together, dance together, talk endlessly. In so doing, they acknowledge themselves as more than just a group of people who happen to have houses in the same neighborhood. Human beings are gregarious. From birth, they require the presence and involvement of adult members of their own species to survive and to learn to live a human life. Most continue relying on the presence and the involvement of others to preserve that way of life. Living together does not necessarily imply liking one another, although it certainly makes life smoother and more pleasant. In any case, all societies have developed ways of greasing the wheels of social interaction so that people will continue to do what is deemed necessary for organized group life to continue, whether they like one another or not.

In many societies around the world, it is the kinship system that positions people within a web of rights and obligations that define who they are and what they must do so that life as they know it may continue. In other societies, social class, religion, ethnic or local traditions, or the power of the state itself enmesh people in structures that make social life possible. In the United States, however, we believe that communities are—and should be—created by the voluntary decisions of individuals. In the early 1970s, the French anthropologist Hervé Varenne lived among the residents of a small town in Wisconsin that he calls Appleton (a pseudonym, although there is a real Appleton, Wisconsin). He observed that the model for social relationships held by people in Appleton, and probably throughout the United States, is based on the freedom of each person to join with other persons to interact in a satisfying, acceptable, and equal way. "In native terms, 'individuals' create 'communities' by congregating with other individuals whom they decide to consider as similar to themselves." Varenne quotes the American philosopher, John Dewey, who wrote that people "live in communities in virtue of the things which they have in common; and communication is the way they come to possess things in common" (Varenne 1977, 157; Dewey, 1966, 4).

Festivals provide individuals with something in common. Although people always talk about the anonymity and isolation of big cities, it is striking how few things exist even in small towns that provide for commonality. Those things that we frequently think of—family, religion, politics—while they create communities, do not create a community that encompasses everyone who lives in a small town. Even humorist Garrison Keillor's Lake Wobegon has two churches! Politics on both the national and state levels separates people, as do local issues such as school referenda and other funding initiatives. Citizens in small Minnesota communities take different positions on abortion, school prayer, censorship, national defense. The local high school sports teams may serve as a common focus, but not everyone in town is interested. Furthermore, the process of regional school consolidation over the last couple of decades in Minnesota has assigned to the high school team an identity that is often separate from that of the community in which the students and their families live.

Under these circumstances, it is often only the festival that is left to recognize and affirm community identity. (This is not to suggest that everyone necessarily likes or agrees about the festival; they do not. It does mean that the festival may come to stand for the most inclusive community.) When asked, festival organizers give several reasons other than building community for putting on the festival: to give something back to the community, to stimulate business, to have fun, to give people something to do, to raise money for civic organizations, to recognize the festival organizers.

But in pursuit of these goals, the festival draws attention to the townspeople themselves. The festival lays claim, in the name of the people of the community, to the entire city: streets, parks, schools, and downtown businesses. It turns these areas over to ordinary members of the community with the blessing of the usual masters of those places: the city, the school district and teachers, the highway department, and local businesses. Regular citizens draw attention to themselves, celebrate themselves: "Look at us. This is our parade, our queen pageant, our way of having fun, our town, our people." Indeed, the festival creates a space—an architecture—in town that is all its own. From the temporary food stands erected by the Youth Hockey, Young Lutherans, Democratic Farmer Labor Party, or Lions Club, to the ball field made queen's court, the parking lot transformed into a carnival, and the streets blocked off for the 10-K run, street dance, or parade, festivals define space in memorable ways. As space is transformed by a parade, the crowd at a street dance, or vast numbers of parked cars, the passage of people through town creates yet another separation of the festival from the daily routine and from the nonfestive use of space. Nowhere is this reversal clearer than when streets are closed for parades, dances, or the carnival. It is as though the people have taken back their city from the practical pursuit of commerce and the facelessness, isolation, and danger of cars—and they take extraordinary pleasure in doing so.

Eating Together

Scholars have long recognized the significance of commensality, or eating together. It is said that in some ancient societies, the laws of hospitality were such that if men had broken bread with each other, even if they were mortal enemies, they were bound together and could not kill each other. A ritual meal shared with others is at the heart of both Judaism (the Passover Seder) and Christianity (the Eucharist). Less sacred, perhaps, but still central to our social lives, are having lunch together, inviting friends for dinner, and being invited to dinner at the homes of friends. The act of eating together has a certain intimacy and informality that helps connect people to each other. Perhaps the festival meal logic is as follows: ordinarily the people with whom I eat are my family; when I extend this ritual to close friends, they become like family; when I eat with people from my town at our festival, they, too, become like family. The communal meal becomes a metaphor for the closeness of the community. Just because the meal is bratwurst, coleslaw, baked beans, and brownies does not mean it is any less meaningful than a formal dinner or religious meal.

Consider the Cokato Corn Carnival, one of the several free corn feeds that are prominent in mid- and late-August festivals. Cokato is a town of twenty-two hundred, located about 50 miles west of Minneapolis. The Cokato Corn Carnival takes place on a Tuesday and Wednesday in mid-August. It is a festival clearly and intentionally for the people of Cokato and its surrounding area, and for people who maintain their connections with Cokato. It is hard to attract tourists from any distance in the middle of the week. With only one 3.2 percent beer bar in the entire town, few in their early twenties from surrounding towns will show up.

For Corn Carnival, 18 tons of sweet corn are brought into town, along with 150 pounds of butter and enough salt, pepper, and waxed paper to satisfy the crowds of corn lovers. On Tuesday afternoon, a large, old tractor with a huge steam boiler is parked on the street on the south side of the park. The boiler is fired up, and a hose is attached to a faucet on the side of the boiler. The other end of the hose goes into an immense water tub located in a permanent shelter. Corn has been cooked in this part of the park since the 1940s. Shucked ears of corn are loaded into a steel basket suspended by pulleys above the tub. When the water is hot enough, the men who cook the corn lower the basket into the tub. Other men move into action, pouring melted butter on metal-topped counters on which the cooked ears of corn will be prepared. Soon the corn is ready. It is just about five in the afternoon, and a long line has formed at the entrance to the shelter. The basket of cooked corn moves along rollers to the counters. Ready hands tip it onto the counter, and the ears of hot corn tumble into the melted butter. Men with rubber gloves roll the ears in the butter. The line begins to move. As people get to the head of the line, they tell the workers how much corn they would like. Each ear is wrapped in waxed paper and handed over. Some people exit immediately to find a place to sit on the grass in the park. Others move to the salt and pepper counters to prepare the corn to taste. The whole process is smooth and efficient. People on both sides of the counters know what they are doing.

The line moves steadily into the shelter. Knots of people sit in the park eating corn. The corn is excellent: sweet, perfectly boiled, and swimming in butter. The late afternoon is warm, the sun is bright, and the shadows are lovely. The laughter and exuberant shouts of children on the carnival rides, especially the giant slide, drift on the breeze, a soft, agreeable counterpoint to the sounds of the voices at the shelter and the crunch of corn being eaten. Some people have already had dinner at home, but most have come to the park to eat. Many service clubs and nonprofit groups are selling food. The largest food stands are sponsored by churches. Both Lutherans and Catholics have dinner stands set up in shelters, with soft drinks, coffee, lemonade, hamburgers, sandwiches, and a variety of enticing home-baked pies behind the counters. Some people have their corn first, then head over to the church dining shelters. Others do the reverse. No matter. No one is making rules. Many within the large crowd know one another and fall into conversations with neighbors on the corn line, in the park, or at the counters inside the church shelters.

As we walk past the corn line, still moving steadily, I am greeted by a colleague from the university and his wife. They are both Cokato natives, they tell me, and have come back to town for Corn Carnival, as they do nearly every summer. Corn Carnival was really the big thing in the summer when they were children, they remark. From the look of the park, it still is. There is a strong feeling of community here, and not just because the people know one another and are all dining in the same place. They have, together, all received food from the community. They did not have to work for the food; they did not even have to pay for it. For most of them, it is a gift that comes from being part of the Cokato community. By accepting the corn, they are, in a sense, accepting and affirming membership in the community.

What of the outsiders? How do they fit in? Perhaps the answer lies in the way in which commensal meals extend the family. If it is the community that eats together, then those who eat together are the community. Outsiders, visitors to the community, can be incorporated for the day into the community through participation in the ritual. By buying food in the community (or in the case of Cokato, receiving food from the community) and eating with members of the community, they are, at least symbolically, identified with the community. There are many other ways to make this happen, of course. Buying a festival button, for example, is another way of connecting with the community.

Representing Communities

Notice that these are not demanding ways to identify with a community: eating together, buying food, buying a button, lining up for a corn feed. One of the essential features of the festival as it builds community is precisely that it is undemanding. As people attend, eat, dance, and enjoy themselves, they are invited to be part of the community. The festival does not demand that people "stand up" for anything. It does not require sacrifice, significant financial investment, or a public declaration of membership in the community. It is low key, quietly and effortlessly doing its work of community making. Participation is easy. "Come and celebrate with your neighbors and friends," it says. "Come and eat with us. Come and dance. Have a beer. Watch the kids have fun. Enjoy the parade." In this way, people come to meet their neighbors, to see others who live in their town, to feel that this place is home and that they belong there, and to begin to lay down memories that will endure and will bind them to a place and a past.

The bonds that festivals build may not be as strong, as intense, or as enduring as those of religious commitment, legal action, powerful shared experience, or deeply held political or moral action. They do not need to be. In fact, they *cannot* be. If we reflect on Varenne's observation about community, we can see how Americans believe that it is their decision to associate with others. They believe that they are free to become involved or to withdraw. They volunteer, and that is an important word. Small towns have volunteer fire departments and rescue squads. Their citizens volunteer to run for mayor or city council, join service clubs that volunteer their time and effort, and sign up to teach Sunday school, deliver meals-on-wheels, visit the sick, help at the hospital, run the parent-teacher organization auction, or help out at school. If everyone drops out, the community collapses. So community festivals cannot press too hard. They need to make participation easy while reminding people of what they have in common. They are one of several means by which Minnesotans connect with one another, and one of the few things that the residents of a small city do together. They are agreeable, and in today's world, that is a very important and, alas, increasingly rare word.

Whose Community?

I have been using the term *community* as though there were only one community made up of everyone in a small town. But small towns, despite how they might appear from the outside, and despite the inclusive language that is often employed in describing them, are not monolithic. Any town is built up from smaller communities, larger than families but smaller than the entire town. They could be called factions, and in some places, that is precisely what they are. But they do not need to be consciously and contentiously opposed to each other. Within the town, existing groups' interests may be opposing, even though they rarely voice their differences.

What are the different groups in a small town? The downtown businesspeople include owners and managers of stores and of small industries, administrators of various kinds, nursing home and retirement home operators, radio station owners, newspaper owners and editors, bankers, insurance agents, real estate agents,

funeral directors, motel owners, restaurant owners. And there are the professionals, including lawyers, doctors, and clergy. Teachers at the local schools, although
professionals, form a distinct group, frequently separate from all other groups in
the community. Another group, the blue-collar workers, includes custodians,
wage laborers in agricultural or light industrial plants, truck drivers, service station attendants, store employees, waitresses, construction workers, nursing home
and hospital orderlies. There is an identifiable group of retired persons, many formerly farmers who now live in town, and there is a group of young people, mostly
males, who are marginal to the community for essentially economic reasons and
will probably have to leave town to find work. Finally, in the wider community
are the farm families that live outside the town but shop and send their children
to school in town.

Given the sheer weight of numbers alone, it is not surprising that the principal
voice heard in these communities is a combination of those of the business and
professional groups. The other groups tend to go along with that voice, or at least
not to argue much with its claim that it speaks for the entire community, for at
least four reasons. First, the livelihoods of the members of the other groups in
town frequently depend on the health of the business and professional communities, so there is a rather pragmatic reason for agreeing with that community. Second, the things that divide people in a small town are frequently expressed in individual rather than group terms. Someone might claim, "I'm not interested in an
auto swap meet, and you're not interested in the crafts show," instead of saying,
"Our kind of people appreciate craft shows, and *those* people only like auto swap
meets." Third, to some degree there *is* an overlap of interests among the banker,
grocery store manager, auto parts dealer, and construction worker. The men fish
and hunt, follow sports, and so on. As a result, some events of a typical small-
town festival will naturally appeal to many residents of different backgrounds.
There are few, if any, events in most towns that are intended exclusively for one
social class (a cocktail party at a mansion on the lake, for example). Finally, a
small town cannot survive with serious internal rifts. As far as I can tell, most
residents of small towns believe in the concept of community—fellow-feeling, cooperation, and common participation—and will attend events that they believe
build community.

Sometimes, however, rifts occur. These conflicts can take a variety of forms.
Sauk Centre lived through a long and painful struggle between the teachers and
the school board that isolated the teachers to an even greater degree than usual.
The controversy in Glenwood during the mid-1970s over the consumption of alcoholic beverages in public, especially during Waterama, highlighted several different groups with different interests. The middle-class people—many of whom

had recently moved to town, were oriented toward a more urban lifestyle, and saw Waterama as a family event with the possibility of attracting lots of tourists— were in favor of banning alcohol consumption. Younger people, late adolescents in particular, opposed the ban. Those who were more traditional and inward looking saw Waterama as a local event and also opposed the ban. In other communities, the young men are structurally opposed to the older, established businesspeople with regard to employment and access to resources, although the form the opposition tends to take is that the younger people leave the town.

Although most summer community festivals are the product of the work and worldview of the businesspeople, these individuals must, as they organize the festival, think of what interests not only them but the other groups in the community. Occasionally, however, the organizers become so attached to their own ideas and interests that they offend the other groups. In one town, that is precisely what happened. The organizers were so concerned with their own fun that they alienated other community groups, especially those who worked in the town's manufacturing plants. In the opinion of the other groups, the organizers had formed a clique that used the festival for its private parties, made no effort to open some of the festival events to others, and made others feel unwelcome. Those who felt left out not only expressed themselves rather strongly on the subject of the organization to which the festival organizers belonged, they also attended only the parade, skipping the other events. To be sure, most festivals do not fuel, or even reveal, such animosity between groups in a community. Most festivals, however, do exclude older teenage males by providing few if any events of interest to them, and the young men are sometimes rather vocal on the subject.

Most striking, however, is the absence in most festivals of the voice of the rural people. In town after town, the community festival ignores or even actively excludes farmers and events of interest to them. There are no machinery exhibits, no tractor pulls, no animal events, no representatives of farm service organizations, no canning, baking, or fruit and vegetable judging. In some towns, farm interests are no longer even in the parade. This is sometimes not by accident. In the mid-1980s, one festival organizer told me about the plans for the parade. Lowering his voice to a whisper, he confided, "I finally got the last of the damn farm implements out of the parade."

In some festivals, the farmers cannot even attend primary events, which are frequently scheduled for seven o'clock, or milking time on Minnesota dairy farms. When farmers pointed this out to the organizers of one festival, the organizers apologized, affirming that the festival was for everyone. But they have still not changed the time of those events. The county fair is the alternative festival for farmers, who are sometimes quite explicit on this point; they recognize that the community festival is not for them.

Even in those festivals that try to build community based on reference to ethnic heritage, it is ordinarily the ethnic heritage of the dominant group that is accented. In my experience, festivals with ethnic names in Minnesota are no different from festivals with product names or geographic feature names. Kolacky Days is not much different from Turkey Days, and both are similar to Waterama. And although Montgomery celebrates Czech heritage, the majority of residents are of German extraction. When a young woman whose grandparents had come from Ireland was crowned Kolacky Queen one year, she said in her acceptance remarks that she would do the best she could to represent her town, "even though I'm not Czech." "Don't worry," said the Czech-American master of ceremonies in his elaborate Bohemian costume, "if you're from Montgomery, you're Czech!"

Sometimes the tie between the organizers and their festival's ethnic theme is tenuous and even paradoxical. Named by its northern European founders for the capital of Uruguay, and now its sister city, the town of Montevideo, Minnesota, celebrates this unusual tie every year at Fiesta Days, highlighted by the presence of the Uruguayan ambassador or a high-ranking deputy. A wreath is laid at the foot of the statue of José Artigas (a gift from the people of Montevideo, Uruguay, in the 1940s), which stands in a park on Main Street. The queen and her princesses wear Spanish-style lacy dresses with mantillas and combs. There are a few other general Spanish-style touches to the festival and the city's architecture. But in the mid-1980s, the town's Latin American farm-labor pool was not represented in the festival at all.

Festivals, even in small towns, are not untouched by the divisions and disagreements of everyday life. While the divisions between the "us" of the organizers and the "them" of the other groups within the community may be blurred, they are never entirely absent. The festival script put together by the organizers may assert that "we are all one community," but other participants may interpret it as denying their membership in that community.

The festival, both as it is organized and as it works out in practice, becomes public property, creating a public culture. As a result, once the festival starts, it escapes the control of its organizers and becomes subject to the interpretations and actions of its participants and observers. This is what makes festivals exciting, occasionally dangerous, and interesting anthropologically. The openness of the festival as it unfolds affects all the groups that meet in the festival, not just the organizers. Outsiders who attend a small-town festival may find the performance quaint, pretentious, soaked in small-town tradition, or embarrassingly naive, but the community members are equally free to find the outsiders' performance boorish, unpleasant, friendly, or cynical. Rural people and certain groups of young people may find the festival performance exclusionary and, by extension, may see this situation as symbolic of their place in the structure of things in the town. The organizers and their adherents, seeing the withdrawn response of the rural people and what they interpret as the insolence of the young, may decide that the farmers are unsophisticated and the young incorrigible, and act accordingly.

But these are possibilities. It would be just as inaccurate to paint all festivals as rife with hostility, contention, and discrimination as it would be to claim a completely rosy image of them as awash in community, good feeling, and togetherness. There is no one function that all festivals, universally, serve. Rather, depending on the situation in a particular town at a particular moment, a festival can generate hostility or togetherness, or even both at the same time. Because they are undemanding and generally open to a wide range of interests, festivals are likely to encourage feelings of belonging and well-being among participants. That this happens so frequently is a function, I think, of the kinds of communities I have described. But the creation of community does not automatically follow from having a festival. It is not enough to put a festival together and expect a surge in positive community feeling. Both the festival and the feelings of belonging and well-being that are desired take thought and work.

The tractor supplies the steam that boils the water in which the free corn is cooked. Corn Carnival. Cokato.

Corn Carnival, Cokato.

Corn Carnival, Cokato.

Corn Carnival, Cokato.

Corn Carnival, Cokato.

Servers at American Legion breakfast. Kolacky Days, Montgomery.

Sinclair Lewis Days, Sauk Centre.

Kolacky Days, Montgomery.

Sinclair Lewis Days, Sauk Centre.

Sinclair Lewis Days, Sauk Centre.

Kolacky Days, Montgomery.

Early morning before the parade. Watercade, Litchfield.

Awaiting the parade. Sinclair Lewis Days, Sauk Centre.

Awaiting the parade. Pola-Czesky Days, Silver Lake.

Watercade, Litchfield.

Watercade, Litchfield.

Watercade, Litchfield.

Watching the parade. Sinclair Lewis Days, Sauk Centre.

Watching the parade. Watercade, Litchfield.

Precision lawn-chair drill team. Corn Fest, Ortonville.

Rutabaga Festival, Askov.

Rutabaga Festival, Askov.

Watercade, Litchfield.

Watercade, Litchfield.

Kolacky Days, Montgomery.

Selling soft drinks along the parade route. Sinclair Lewis Days, Sauk Centre.

5. HAVING FUN

What does it mean to have fun at a festival? To be fun, an event, performance, or activity has to be pleasurable. It also has to be voluntary in some sense, undemanding, distinctive, and (at festivals) inexpensive or free. Although festivals serve purposes other than just having fun, there are, in fact, many ways of having fun at them. We have already mentioned several of those ways and will here concentrate on three of them—dancing, parade watching, and shopping—each of which represents a different way to enjoy festival activities. Having fun can be public or private, self-conscious or unself-conscious, an everyday affair, or something that comes around only once a year. Shopping is an everyday, unself-conscious activity. We shop frequently and without thinking much about the people around us. Watching a parade is more public and infrequent, but still mostly unself-conscious, as the paradegoers concentrate on watching the parade. Going to a street dance is even more public, relatively infrequent, and quite self-conscious.

Dancing on the Street, Dancing in the Park

At the street dance, people are in public in a way that is not available any other time of the year. Even if they go dancing every weekend, they can only dance where dancing is available—bars, ballrooms, clubs, or a school dance. All of these are bounded spaces, not open to everyone. But contrast that to Kolacky Days in

Montgomery, where all you need is a button to enter the park where the dance takes place. The "dance floor" is the large asphalt area between the bandstand and the edge of the picnic area. There are perhaps a thousand or more people, and you are simultaneously lost in the crowd and free to perform however you wish. Of course, if you are surrounded by people you know, you may be limited in just how far you can push your performance. But suppose you are from Lonsdale or Le Center or New Prague. Montgomery's festival allows you the freedom of relative anonymity. And that is exactly what those in the crowd tell interviewers, for the crowds at dances always include many visitors from other towns.

And why not seek such freedom? After you have spent a long hot day working or just hanging out, a dance in the cool of the evening sounds like a good idea. There have been ads in the county shopper and signs about town, and the featured band is well known in the area. It specializes in mid-sixties tunes and has a local following. So you call a few friends and agree to drive over to Montgomery together. When you arrive, about nine-thirty, things are really hopping. You cruise around, looking for a place to park. A man sitting on his porch offers to let you park on his lawn, and you gratefully accept. You pay your three dollars at the gate for a button, and you are in. Among the crowd you see some people you know, but not too many. The band is playing, the beer is flowing, you and your friends are dancing, and there are a number of attractive people around. You dance and chat with a couple of them.

Suddenly, people are running and craning their necks. A fight has broken out. Two police officers move quickly through the crowd. Suddenly, the fight swirls by you, two very angry and drunken young men pushing and punching. One lands in some bushes, and the other is about to jump on him when the policemen catch up. One officer grabs the one in the bushes; the other officer collars the one who is advancing. The two brawlers, still in a fury, are nearly spitting at each other, trying to get free of the policemen. The officers move them off in different directions, and the excitement is over. "Fighting over a girl, I bet," says one man. "Nah," says another, "the kids from New Prague and Montgomery always get into fights at these things." The band plays on, and the fun continues.

Putting the Community on the Street: The Parade

The pleasures of the dance are evening pleasures, enacted in public. A parade represents a different kind of fun. It is a major public display. In some towns, at the crack of dawn or even the night before, people set up their lawn chairs along the parade route to save themselves good spots. Arriving early in the morning, a visitor to Litchfield is presented with an eerie sight: rows of empty lawn chairs lined up along the curb as though ghostly spectators were watching an invisible parade. By eleven-thirty, traffic into town is heavy and people are parking farther and farther away from the downtown parade area. Experienced visitors are carrying lawn chairs and coolers.

Parades usually begin in residential areas, then turn onto the downtown business streets, where the largest crowds gather, pass through downtown, and then end at a park or school in another residential district. When there is judging of the high school bands, the judges are always located in the center of the business district blocks. The parents of the members of visiting bands wedge themselves in near the judging area because that is where the bands play and march their best. Paradegoers from out of town seem loath to intrude too much in the residential neighborhoods. They pack the public parts of town: the downtown commercial area, the parks, blocks with schools or churches, and intersections. They leave the start and finish to those who live in town or who are visiting friends in town. Respect for the property of others is strong among the people who attend parades.

At twelve-thirty, the crush of people downtown is intense, with more than six hundred on each side of the street per block, according to my students, who have counted them. Vendors are moving purposefully up and down the streets. The hockey team and the swim club are selling soft drinks, and the novelty vendors from the Twin Cities have their shopping carts jammed with horns, big balloons, plastic swords, pennants, inflatable toys, streamers, and all the little souvenirs that are a child's delight and a parent's long sigh. The children are becoming a bit impatient, but they are still behaving, and though it is hot, they are still excited.

At ten after one, sirens can finally be heard. The parade is on its way. Up the street, a police car with all its lights flashing and its siren on, turns onto Main Street. Finally! Behind it comes the American Legion color guard, a group of men squeezed into uniforms that once fit them easily. They are still proud, erect, and marching as sharply as they did thirty-five or forty years ago. On either side of the street, a wave seems to precede them. Everyone rises as the flag passes, men uncover their heads, and hands cover hearts. Only after the flag is well past do they sit again. As the color guard passes the reviewing stand, the commander orders "Eyes, right!" The Minnesota and American Legion flags dip, the commander snaps a salute, the men with the rifles on their shoulders snap their heads to the right. The band judges, in their black slacks, white shirts, and black caps with the judging association's logo, come to attention and salute. They are on the street, ready to assess and score the bands. As the color guard passes, followed by the screaming sirens and deep roar of the air horns from the fire trucks, the band judges spread out across the street, waiting for the host band, the hometown band, to approach.

And here they are. The crowd is cheering as they approach, all eyes directed up the street. The band pauses for a moment. The street beat from the drummers stops. Three sharp whistles and the drum major's baton jerks upward. The drums begin again, this time with the opening of the band's performance music. The two students carrying the band's banner lift it sharply and then bring it down as they move forward into the judging area. The band's color guard, right behind them, move like wooden soldiers, so stiff and so erect. The flag twirlers begin their complex routines, the flags snapping in the still air and the staffs smacking the ground resoundingly from the speed and precision those long hours of practice have given the twirlers' arms. The majorettes are moving into the judging area now, all the batons seemingly connected to each other. The two drum majors, an intensely serious couple, move to the reviewing stand and execute an elaborate salute, throwing their heads back so crisply that one worries about whiplash. And now, the band itself moves in front of the reviewing stand. The judges are weaving an elaborate counterpoint to the band, as they watch here, run there, examine the marching, listen critically to the sounds. The band sounds good this year; the new director has done wonders for it. The uniforms that were purchased a couple of years ago are still smart looking, and the spats make everyone aware that they really have their marching together. Look at those feet—up and down together with nearly perfect precision. Even the small student with the huge sousaphone is right with the others. The band assistants with the buckets of ice chips are alongside now, watching to see if any of the musicians need cooling down, but they are all intent on what they are doing. The trumpet soloist steps out and plays. She sounds better here at home than she did last week in Foley. This is music that only sounds good live. The camcorder microphone cannot catch it well and causes it to sound tinny and out of tune. The mixture of sounds from the instruments seems to blend successfully only as the band moves toward the listener and then away. To great applause, the band marches out of the judging area as the musicians crisply snap their instruments into rest position. The drum line shifts to the street beat, and off they go. Already, eyes are turning back up the street.

The first float appears. It is the local float, carrying the town queen and princesses. The young women wave, and some of the children wave back. Most people just watch, which is generally their only reaction to the parade units, with the exception of the high school bands and a few unusual floats. Otherwise, paradegoers seem to think of themselves as spectators rather than participants. They simply watch most of the units go by. They do not cheer, applaud, or interact with the parade units. It is almost as though television has so conditioned them to expect a barrier between the event and themselves that they can only respond with passive spectatorship at live events until something—the local high school band, recognizing someone on a float, a patriotic appeal—shakes them out of it.

I was able to observe an interesting contrast in paradegoing styles in 1991. I accompanied a group of Costa Ricans visiting Minnesota to Pola-Czesky Days in Silver Lake, a town of 760 people in central Minnesota. Most of those along the parade route seemed content to watch as passively as any Minnesota parade crowd. Not the Costa Ricans! They waved at everyone who waved at them, they rushed into the street to pose with royalty on floats, they laughed, they interacted, they made themselves part of the parade. The people on the floats were a bit taken aback at first when the Costa Ricans started interacting with them, but enjoyed the Costa Ricans' spirit of festivity. There was a sense that having fun involved not just spectatorship but, in a spirit of celebration, immersing oneself in the event, entering in and becoming part of the fun rather than standing off and watching.

There are different ways to have fun at parades, and the meaning of *parade* is clearly something that varies from place to place. How you take your pleasure and how you engage yourself in an event like a parade—whether you sit back and watch or get involved—are not just individual characteristics. People learn to be Minnesotans in a number of different ways, and they display their "Minnesotaness" in various contexts. Standing and watching a parade in an orderly, polite, calm, yet interested and friendly way is simultaneously a way of learning how to behave in public and a demonstration that you know how to behave at a parade.

But the parade is still on the street. Festival organizers in convertibles are going by, along with the mayor, state legislators, and the grand marshal. Floats from different towns in the region, each carrying the community queen and her princesses, all waving together and smiling, pass by. Several parades have over thirty royalty floats in them, nearly one-third of the units in the parade. Clowns come by, some interacting with the crowd and doing their tricks with individual audience members, others performing their routines as they march together in the middle of the road. I have been struck by the number of late middle-aged women who have gone into clowning recently. Old videotapes and photographs from the early 1980s do not show near the number of clowns, clown clubs, and clown groups in parades that one finds these days. Perhaps the economic difficulties and the pressures of leading an ordinary life in small towns in the late 1980s and early 1990s inspire certain individuals to find relief in the anonymous anarchy of the clown. Something needs to be fun in people's lives.

The first group of horses goes by, followed by the cleanup crew. The children love it when the horses obey the call of nature. They love it even more when the cleanup crew rushes into action moments before the next band appears. We will see not only these horses today but several riding clubs, Percherons and Belgians pulling wagons, miniature ponies, two huge oxen ("2½ tons of Brute Power," we read in the parade brochure handed us on the street), a llama pulling a small carriage, and trained dogs. Different parade committees have different strategies for the animal units. Some just work them in with the other units in the parade, striving for a balance of different units throughout. Others, more cautious, place all the animals at the end of the parade, after the last marching units.

Following another band, a couple of royalty floats, and the first 4-H float, the first set of classic and antique cars rolls past. There are twenty-five of them, ranging from a Ford Model T, Plymouths from the 1930s and 1940s, and late 1950s Thunderbirds to more recent models. There will be more cars in the parade later—hot rods, old cars, convertibles, and many other vehicles. Some parades even send semitrailers from local trucking companies down the street, along with snowmobiles on trailers, tractors, and the immense agricultural implements that have so transformed mechanized farming. The heavy equipment, in the parades that feature it, makes an overwhelming impression. By their gargantuan size, these great machines are symbols of power. But they are also concrete emblems of the productive capacity and inventive engineering of American industry and of the economic success of a community that can afford to sell and buy such equipment. In bad economic times, the marshaling of this equipment almost seems to be a talisman protecting the town from the forces that threaten it.

But there are no generic parades. Parades are specific to the towns they are in, and they vary in their makeup in interesting and important ways. How a parade is put together is a combination of several factors: the parade's date (these days most high school bands stop marching after the Minneapolis Aquatennial in late July), how early the organizers start contacting units (some get booked very early), other parades the organizers have been to ("we saw a real cute float in Paynesville last summer"), the organizers' own tastes as socially situated persons ("we finally got the last of the farm machinery out of the parade"), the things that interest people in their community (the Sons of Norway float is popular in some parts of the state, and heavy equipment, farm machinery, and draft animals are popular in some rural communities), and the things and people that communities are proud of (in 1991, Operation Desert Storm veterans were highlighted in parades, as were members of the Vietnam Veterans of America. I have also seen in parades high school basketball teams that did well at the state level, new trucks for the fire department or private enterprises in town, and floats made by, or featuring, the town's children). The result of these factors in any town is a parade that is different from any other parade in the state in terms of what it highlights or what is absent. It is a parade that says something to the people of the town about their world and what matters in it. Out of such apparently humble, commonplace elements as fire trucks, semitrailers, antique cars, bands, clowns, candy thrown from floats, square dancers, old-time musicians on flatbeds, 4-H floats, llamas pulling carts, community queens, dairy princesses, and pork industry queens are built up our most deeply held pictures of what our community is like.

Even the end of a parade is important. Some parades have what could be called inclusive endings. People along the parade route join the parade, falling in after the last units and walking with them to the park where the parade ends. There they picnic, dance, go to the carnival, or wait for other events to begin. There is a sense of participation and of festivity. There are other communities in which there is no such "people's parade." The parade ends at an intersection or across a busy highway, or people just walk away, back to their cars after the parade has passed by. Regardless of how they end, parades provide spectacle, a sense of a community, a region on display, and a feeling for the richness and complexity of the world in which the people of the region live.

Shopping: The Pleasures of Looking and Buying

From the souvenirs along the parade route to the arts and crafts show, from the flea market to the crazy days sales, festivals provide many opportunities to shop and to spend money. The crazy days sales found in many communities are handled in a couple of different ways. Crazy days shopping offers everyday goods at excellent prices, but merchants in many communities also use crazy days to get rid of clearance merchandise or things that they have had in the storeroom for years. Other merchants bring in new, inexpensive merchandise that they have never carried before. This provides a double advantage. The merchants make a nice profit from the new material, and shoppers in town are delighted with the new selection offered at such excellent prices. Merchants put their goods out on the sidewalk in front of the store, lending a festive atmosphere to the shopping, giving Main Street the air of a market in another part of the world, and also making it easier for shoppers to view and select the goods presented. People do buy. Mostly women, but men, too, peer intently at the clothing, toys, hardware, pictures, photo albums, checking for flaws and asking for different sizes.

My students were avid crazy days shoppers. They were curious at first about why many stores with large crazy days promotions were closed on the Sunday of the parade. They assumed that this would be the ideal time to open: the crowds in town were the largest of the entire festival, and many people would be attracted by the bargains. What storekeepers told me was a different story. Crowds that big were dangerous and shoplifting might increase. There were so many people in town that the outdoor displays would only be in the way of people interested in watching the parade, and goods might be knocked over and dirtied or broken. Besides, the people coming to town for the parade were there for the parade and to look at arts and crafts, not to shop for dresses or posters or Minnesota Vikings jerseys. Anyway, if they opened, they and their employees would miss the parade! Most important of all, perhaps, was the explanation that the crazy days sales were for the trade area, for the people who patronized the stores all year long. It was a way for the merchants to thank the local people by offering these goods to them exclusively.

The other kind of festival shopping is done at flea markets and arts and crafts fairs, which offer items not ordinarily found in the downtown shops. A memorable crafts fair was at the 1991 Kolacky Days in Montgomery. Spread out through the park on a day that threatened rain was a broad range of items. At one table, a man who had made many trips to Czechoslovakia was selling genealogical information and books in Czech. A woman next to him was selling T-shirts and sweatshirts from universities in what was then still Czechoslovakia, as well as booklets on Czech-American topics. A couple of women nearby were selling beautiful handmade lace. Several other stands had been set up from which people were selling crafts fair standbys such as quilted or chintz animals, carved name plaques for babies' bedrooms, macramé hangers, plaques with inspirational messages. One retired couple had set up a stand to sell wind catchers. These were green plastic two-liter soft drink bottles out of which they had cut thin spiral sections. When the bottles were hung on a string, the slightest breeze set them turning. Other bottles had been cut vertically, and a little bird perch with a toy bird sitting on it was placed inside. There was a man who built wooden rocking toys for children. Another table displayed the work of a folk artist from the area who made wonderfully clever biplanes out of beverage cans. The propellers spun in the wind. They came in a variety of sizes, and shoppers could choose according to their favorite brand of beer, juice, or soft drink. Another table had been set up by two Russian women who were selling toy cars, airplanes, tanks, medals, sports club pins, small dolls—all from the former Soviet Union. People were curious, but the prices were high and the women did not seem to be selling much.

Other crafts fairs are more elaborate, with stands for potters, jewelry makers, woodworkers, painters, and other types of craftspeople. Some festivalgoers seem to be doing early Christmas shopping, but my overall impression is that sales are slow at most of these fairs. People look a lot but do not buy much. The fun is in the browsing, maybe finding one or two things that would look nice on the hutch or in the children's room or for Aunt Jane.

The same seems to be true at flea markets, although the average age of the vendors and the shoppers is much older than at most other festival shopping events.

Festival flea markets display a staggering array of stuff, from old car parts to ancient kitchen tools and valuable depression-era glassware and dishes. There are
books to be pored over, postcards to look through, hardware to sift. Like the
craftspeople, the flea market vendors make a circuit through the region during
the summer, seeing each other regularly, often visiting with people they have met
in town during their previous travels. Many of the flea market vendors are retired,
driving large recreational vehicles from flea market to flea market, living in the vehicles, and having a wonderful time. What many of them seem to enjoy most are
the conversations they strike up with the people their own age who recognize
what they are selling. It is fun for them and fun for the shoppers. Everyday shopping at stores that one has patronized for years loses some of its excitement, but
the fun of shopping at a festival is precisely its unpredictability. That is what
makes new, large shopping malls such desirable places to shop. They are not util-
itarian; they do not offer the same old stuff; they make shopping fun again.

The shopping is thus like other parts of a Minnesota summer festival; it is out
of the ordinary, pleasurable in a variety of ways, and out of doors. The dance and
the shopping are both usually indoor events taken outside at this unusual time;
the parade must be outdoors and is so central to the definition of a festival that it
is the event most likely to be found in any Minnesota festival.

There is yet another way of having fun at Minnesota festivals—a way that is a
bit rowdy, perhaps even a little frightening. It is the traveling carnival.

6. CARNIVAL!

The first sign that something is happening is when the campers and a recreational vehicle arrive in town, followed by a caravan of trucks carrying trailers, equipment, and rides folded up like great gawky birds. The carnival has arrived in town. Young men step down from the trucks. The owner steps out of the RV. He does not have to tell them much; they have been doing this all summer, and maybe a lot longer. The men wear blue jeans and dirty T-shirts; some have tattoos on their arms. They need shaves, and their long, greasy hair flows from underneath caps advertising Harley-Davidson or Led Zeppelin. It looks as though they have been on the road a long time.

The rides start going up—Tilt-a-Whirl, Ferris wheel, Hurricane, carousel, kiddie rides. Electrical cables snake all over the ground, leading to generators. The generators cough a couple of times and then roar to life. A ticket booth goes up. The sides of trailers are lifted to reveal carnival games—ringtoss, shooting gallery, frog pond, darts and balloons. Several women are arranging the prizes and setting up the cigarette boxes, the bottles, the frogs, the little cranes. Cotton candy and popcorn stands, soda pop and minidonut machines, go up. One man who appears to be in his thirties has a large crescent wrench, a scowl, and grease all over him as he tries to fix the gears on the Tilt-a-Whirl. It is taking him a long time. Another man goes over to help him. Finally, they are done. Guardrails and low fences to keep people away and in line for the rides are in place. The carnies disappear—some to campers, some downtown, and some to the high school, where the locker rooms have been opened for them so they can clean up.

60

The carnival is ready! It opens tonight, and the festival starts tomorrow. For the past two weeks, carnival tickets have been on sale in town, and posters have been up for nearly a month. The local paper has been running articles about where tickets may be purchased and how much cheaper they are when bought in advance. But sales have not been great. People are ambivalent about the carnival.

They have always been ambivalent about the carnival. There is even a classic American musical that hinges on that ambivalence—*Carousel*. But now, things are even worse for the traveling carnivals. Once, they were central to summertime entertainment, carrying with them hints of disorder, sleaze, and danger, along with the exciting rides and the opportunity to play games of chance. But in today's Minnesota, permanent amusement parks like Valley Fair or Knott's Camp Snoopy, as well as Indian casinos, the state lottery, charitable gambling, and drugs and crime, have removed much of the allure of the traveling carnival. Liability insurance, drug laws, and state licensing have each had a part to play, too.

Valley Fair, in particular, has done its job very well. It sometimes seems that every child in the state has been to Valley Fair, and most more than once. School districts and youth groups of every kind from all over the state plan trips there as special treats for the children. Valley Fair puts its advertisements on television and on billboards. For many families, the children insist on at least one trip per year to Valley Fair. The rides are wonderful—scary, massive, built into the earth itself—and there are more than thirty of them. Once you are in at Valley Fair, all you have to do is go stand in line. Most of the rides are included in the cost of admission; you do not need a handful of tickets. Nine places to eat, plus refreshment stands, are scattered throughout the grounds. And the restrooms are not portable. There's entertainment, too. The staff, which numbers over one thousand, are well groomed, friendly young people of the sort you would like to have living next door. A day at Valley Fair is expensive, but the children love it.

What chance does a traveling carnival have to compete? Its handful of small rides, by comparison, sometimes looks rickety and unsafe, even though they may be tested regularly. In 1984, I was walking down the main street in Montevideo on the first day of Fiesta Days. Behind me were a sister and brother, about eight and eleven years old, talking about the carnival. They were discussing how much it cost, how they had to have tickets for all the rides, and how that was not like Valley Fair. They agreed that the rides at Valley Fair were much better and decided to save most of their allowances for the trip to Valley Fair, some 125 miles away. There are fewer traveling carnivals these days, and the crowds they draw seem to be smaller than they were ten years ago.

When I first started studying festivals in Minnesota, there were no charitable gambling, no state lottery, no casinos on Indian reservations. Carnivals provided games of chance, contests in which you might win something, the feeling that you were gambling. The prizes, then as now, were stuffed animals, posters, little trinkets. Modern state-sponsored gambling is much more lucrative, and it takes the money that people might previously have used at the carnival games.

What the traveling carnival brings is a sense of danger and raffishness, of the exotic and the out-of-control. This is conveyed through the people who work for the carnival. They are regarded as tough, mean, dangerous, and possibly even criminals on the run. The carnies encourage these beliefs through their scruffy appearance. They refuse to give real names, preferring nicknames; and they scowl and talk tough, threatening people who try to take their photograph. Sometimes what people believe about them is true, but the tough image also keeps people at a distance so that the carnies can do their jobs. Students who have worked with me on this research have observed how many young women are attracted by the carnies, sometimes even talking about running away with the carnival when it leaves town. The lure of the carnival is strong. It simultaneously provides anonymity and family, allowing its people to create themselves as they wish, to play, to travel, but mostly to break free. For adolescents, especially young women who feel that they face little more than a tough time in a small town with no jobs, the same old boring people, and no way out, the carnival represents freedom.

The drawback to this image is that it attracts the police, who watch the carnies carefully. Worse, the image also brings out the young men with a little beer in them ready to prove how tough *they* are by getting into fights with the toughest men who come through town, the carnies. Sometimes the carnies are ready to fight, but usually they are not. In 1985, the townie-carny fight in one of the towns I studied resulted in a group of young men beating up a lone carny in a local bar, where he had gone to have a beer and relax after the carnival had closed for the night.

At a meeting of festival organizers in Montevideo in 1984, some local women told of an incident the year before, when one of the carnies robbed a store and knifed a local youth. After the meeting, a police officer took us aside and explained that the young man who had been stabbed was mostly scared. The cut was not too deep, he said, and the offender was kept in Montevideo for a while. He spent part of that time at the officer's home, where the officer and his wife got to know him. He could not read or write, and he had felt that he was being attacked by a whole crowd of young men and did the only thing he could. The officer was quite sympathetic, but, of course, the impression of carnival people held by most of the townspeople was probably closer to that of the women who had originally told us of the incident.

Paradoxically, such incidents make the carnival and its people much more interesting. They add a strong note of "them" to the festival—and not a good "them" like the out-of-town tourists that communities like to attract—but they are necessary for the festival. They make the good people of the community think better of themselves and the choices they have made in their lives, but they also add a note of exciting disorder to what is otherwise an orderly festival held in an orderly community. After an entire year of order and fellowship, the lure of the carnival is almost overwhelming to many people.

Carnival, the Carnivalesque, and the Small Town

Scholars often talk about carnival, but what they mean is rather different from the traveling carnival. They are referring, instead, to the pre-Lenten celebration of disorder that is still practiced in Latin America (famously in Brazil, especially Rio de Janeiro) and parts of Europe and that still survives in Mardi Gras in New Orleans. The classic Carnival (which I will distinguish with an uppercase C) dates back at least as far as the Middle Ages in Europe and was celebrated on the three days prior to Ash Wednesday. These were three days of riotous celebration, a time of license and of being able to get away with things forbidden at other times of the year. Celebrants would make fun of those in power, when, for a moment, they had power. Dressed in costumes, they went to parades and parties and did a lot of drinking. Those who were low were raised up. The poor and the dispossessed took over towns and cities, parodying the upper and middle classes, throwing water and paint at bystanders, and otherwise carrying on. It was the time of the ordinary people, freed for a moment from the power of the social hierarchy that held them in place throughout the year and to which they would return with the solemnity of Ash Wednesday and Lent. Anthropologists refer to events of this sort as "rites of reversal," wherein everything is turned upside down, tensions are momentarily relaxed, those with power feel what powerlessness is like, and those without power can revel in their freedom.

It was a strange and dangerous time, one in which people laughed at the trappings and pretensions of power that bound them and that they could not escape. The great Russian literary theorist Mikhail Bakhtin writes that the laughter of Carnival is ambivalent. "It is gay, triumphant, and at the same time mocking, deriding. It asserts and denies, it buries and revives. . . . the people's ambivalent laughter . . . expresses the point of view of the whole world; he who is laughing also belongs to it" (Bakhtin 1968, 11–12). This is the essential act of Carnival: that its humor is ambivalent and reflexive. Carnival is beyond good or bad, always containing the threat of violence, of overthrow, but also the possibility of openness, of reconstructing communities in ways they may not have been structured before. Through this playfulness, which draws attention to alternatives, the structure of the society is called into question.

This is the threat and promise of Carnival. In medieval Europe, the threat of Carnival was controlled, since the structure of the medieval world—the ties that bound people to one another—was based on kinship, feudal or class relations, religion, and long-term, unchangeable residence. In a great city of the present day, people can run away and never see each other again. But a full-bore Carnival of this kind would be devastating in a small town in the United States. The town would be ripped apart. Why? Because we Americans act on the assumption that we *voluntarily* come together as equals to form communities made up of people who live in the same town. We believe that we associate together because we need each other and, ultimately, because we want to. But just as we can decide to associate, we can decide to withdraw. If worse comes to worst, we can move to another town.

Imagine the scene the day after Carnival if you lived in a small town in Minnesota. Walking into the supermarket, the hardware store, the clinic, you would have to face the people on whom you threw paint, whose lifestyle you had burlesqued for three days, who saw you falling down drunk singing vulgar songs about the school board. One of them is *on* the school board. Not that everyone else's behavior was all that much better. You think you recognize who was with your boss's husband throughout Carnival. The young attendant at the gas station behaved so rudely that you refuse to buy gas there anymore. Three school board members resigned after hearing the songs, claiming that they certainly had no intention of putting up with that kind of abuse for trying to help out the community. You see what the problems with Carnival would be. If we consider ourselves fundamentally equal individuals with the capacity to choose to participate in or withdraw from community life, an event like Carnival would reveal not the strong and multiple structures that hold society together but rather the chaos that lies beneath the orderly surface of American small-town social relations.

So that leaves the traveling carnival and its carnies. That much disorder and uncertainty can be handled—it is even a bit exciting. And they are outsiders—by definition and by desire. Once they are gone, things go back to normal.

The Carnival Comes to Life

But now it is seven in the evening, and the lights at the carnival go on. The red, green, white, and electric blue of the neon lights on the rides begin to swirl as the first rides begin. Above the canvas fronts of the games, the yellow and white bulbs are switched on, hardly visible against the setting sun. The younger children are arriving with their parents. They ride the merry-go-round, the carousel, the little cars. Some try the Ferris wheel. They try the games, too, and so do their fathers. This is usually an easy and pleasant time, and it is something for a young family to do in the evening. Some evenings, there are quite a few of them, some with a very little one in the stroller, one on dad's shoulders, and another running ahead.

Sometimes, though, even during "kiddie time," things can turn unpleasant. A young mother of two little girls, seven and four, told one of my students in 1987 that the carnival in 1986 had been better. "The carnies were clean-cut kids who helped the children get on the rides, which were in better condition, freshly painted. This year, they acted like they didn't want us around. They were grody and said some obscene things to me when Bill [her husband] wasn't there, but the little girls were. It made me mad." Her seven-year-old daughter remarked that there were not many people there when they had gone on the rides; she had not seen anyone she recognized. This is why carnies have be especially careful during these hours. Their business depends on what mothers and fathers tell one another about the carnival. If the parents are offended, business drops off. If they are pleased, the carnival will be crowded and everyone will be pleased.

By nine o'clock, the little children are gone, replaced by the high school students. It is nearly dark now, and the lighted rides really stand out against the night sky. As the rides twirl, lift, and drop, the colored neon lights on them make almost hallucinatory patterns in the deepening dark. The bulbs on the games and on the carnival paths have transformed the entire area. It looks different, almost golden, and inviting. The carnies in the shows are in full voice, attracting customers with their well-practiced lines. Several couples are in the carnival area now, mostly middle to late teens. The boys are showing off to their girlfriends, with rifles on shoulders, aiming at the trinkets; darts poised, aiming at the balloons; pitching arms cocked to knock down the wooden milk bottles at three balls for a dollar. The minidonuts, one of the real treats in the festival, are selling well. The Hurricane, the Tilt-a-Whirl, and all the wild rides are going full blast. The shriek of teenage girls is heard throughout the evening air. Teenage boys, terminally cool, try hard not to look scared.

It is closer to ten o'clock now. The queen pageant has just ended, and young women in formal gowns—the local candidates and the visiting royalty from other communities—flood the carnival. They love the rides, spinning through the air in long dresses and crowns, squealing in joyful terror. It looks so incongruous, these formally attired young women in traveling carnival rides. But they are enjoying themselves so much! If there is one image that seems to sum up the festival, this is it. The most ritualistic, controlled part of the festival juxtaposed with the freest

and most chaotic. Neither is more important than the other; they are both ele-
mental in festivals. But it is here that they embrace each other in formal-garbed
giddiness.

Now the carnies are in their element. At this point in the evening, being tough,
slightly threatening, and rude are competitive advantages. Many of the carnies,
male and female, game operators and ride operators, are masters of the come-on,
the carefully chosen line to attract the unwary. This is not the stereotypic, turn-of-
the-century "Step right up, ladies and gentlemen, to see the seventh wonder of the
world." Some of these people are so good that their marks do not even know they
are being fed a line (which, of course, is the whole point). Even researchers are not
immune. In 1987, Deborah Green, a student, interviewed and observed one of the
ride operators.

This man looks like he would be in his 30s, but he shows me his I.D. and is actually 26. He has a kind of weathered look, with long hair and beard that I assume
to be intentionally misleading. His I.D. picture, taken only 6 months ago, clean
shaven and with short hair, looks much younger than his age.

He closes the door of a plane ride on three males (16–18 years old) and yells at
them: "Shut up. Don't say a word."

One male says, "Mums the word."

"But you can scream if you want." They laugh.

I ask him how long he has been an entertainer.

"I've been a carny for 10 years."

"But you entertain them as well as give them rides."

"It helps them while they are up on the rides. If they are afraid of me they don't
think about being afraid of the ride and it keeps them from puking. It also keeps
them sitting in their seats the way they are supposed to, because these rides could
be dangerous. I had this kid one time standing up and I had to kick him off."

I ask him if he has a lot of problems with high school boys.

"Some, but nothing I can't handle."

He tells me that the carnies do all their own maintenance on their rides; putting
up and taking down, greasing and fixing them. He worked the game booths up until 6 months ago: "That's how come I act so crazy." I think that is how he learned
to be such a smooth talker. "I'm writing a book of poetry. I only went to school to
the ninth grade, but there are famous writers who didn't need school; you know
that guy who wrote Romeo and Juliet."

"You mean Shakespeare?"

"Yeah, he only went to the third grade."

"Oh, I didn't know that. What do you do during the winter when you can't work
for the carnival?"

"I go up to the mountains in Montana."

"How about money?"

"Don't need none. I hunt and fish. I love the outdoors. I have my own cabin up there."

"I'm asking you these questions because I'm studying social control, and there are a lot of different ways of controlling people."

"Oh, I have my own control."

"So I see."

He talks them into believing he is tough, but could be their friend if they listen and do what he says. . . .

He also says to me, "Hope you're not upset because I don't have the pin you gave me." (I gave him a "Number 1" pin earlier that day after riding the Hurricane for the best ride at the carnival. It made my connection for the interview.) "I gave it away to this retarded boy when he was crying because his parents wouldn't let him ride, then he smiled all the way out of here."

"Good, that's great."

The ride operator's rhetoric is interesting here. His "line" to the teenagers at the beginning is an example of the practical uses of intimidation and humor; he can keep the ride running efficiently only if riders follow the rules. His explanation of this strategy makes the interview sound entirely informational. But at the same time, he finds several different ways to tell the interviewer that he is tough, that he has power.

Most striking is the way he seems to be manipulating the interviewer. This begins when he suddenly speaks of writing poetry. The interviewer has already identified herself as a college student, and the ride operator seems to be using that information as he directs the conversation. He might actually write poetry (it seems that everyone does these days), but even if he is not a writer, poetry would seem to be an attractive subject to a college woman. He certainly would not be likely to start talking about poetry with a police officer wandering about the carnival. He is also implying that his lack of education does not mean he is not creative; she may go to college, but he writes poetry. He follows this with the romantic image of his isolated cabin in Montana and his ability to live off the land, and then comes the rhetorical masterstroke at the end.

At the end of the interview notes, it is the ride operator, not the interviewer, who raises the issue of the missing button. What could be more sentimentally heartwarming than the story he tells her? The tough carny with the heart of gold, giving the button to a mentally handicapped child whose parents refuse to allow him on the ride. What better way to get the sympathy of a friendly college woman? It could be true. But it could also be part of the constant creation of self, the attempt to fit with whomever one is speaking to, that is part of the freedom and joy of the carnival life.

It is getting late now, close to midnight. The sparse crowd looks a little older now and maybe a little rougher. Sometimes, fights break out late in the evening. The joy of *ilinx*, vertigo, the whirling giddiness of the carnival ride, seems reduced late in the evening, and a sadness seems to pervade the carnival as the carnival workers, tired now, perhaps disappointed, stand at their stations, waiting for the night to be over. Finally, the motors are shut down and the lights switched off on the last rides. Several have been off for nearly an hour. The game shows are closed down. Some of the carnies slip downtown to one of the bars or another for a drink. Many head for their campers, some alone, others hoping that the whispered words and meaningful glances exchanged earlier in the day mean that they will not be alone for long. The carnival is over for another night.

7. PUTTING IT ON

S mall-town festivals do not just happen. The apparent spontaneity and simplicity of a festival as it unrolls over the course of a few days are the product of an enormous amount of work and a significant level of organization. Festivals in Minnesota are organized in many different ways, but most forms of organization fall along a continuum, the ends of which can be called "family style" and "corporate style."

Family-Style Organization

Family-style organization is so called because there is a long-term principal organizer who takes on the role of "parent" to the festival and to other organizers. This person may or may not be paid, but in either case, the person has made a long-term commitment to the festival. It can be someone who just loves festivals, someone who handles organization extremely well, or someone who is willing to do the job when no one else will. All activity connected with running the festival is directed or coordinated by the principal organizer. Other people who get involved in the festival know only the details connected with their own event. How that event fits with other events or how other events are organized is a mystery to them. In some cases, the principal organizer is the only person who knows how all the details of the festival come together.

Family-style organization can make for a very efficient festival. One person who is willing and able to do the work can accomplish a great deal. It is the festival organizer who sends out the letters inviting animal units, high school bands, clown clubs, car clubs, and all the rest to be in the parade, who sends the call for queen pageant candidates to the local paper, who decides which traveling carnival should be invited, and who makes sure that the traveling carnival has been contacted in good time. The principal organizer buys materials for the kiddie-day events, gets the parade permit, handles the details of food stands, coordinates with the police and state patrol. Part of the job of principal organizer is also to ask friends and acquaintances in town to help out. "They always do, because they know I don't ask unless I need them," said one organizer. Helpers are delegated a specific task—to line up the parade, to decorate the gym for the queen pageant, to obtain volunteers for the beer garden, to set up for the street dance.

The result of family-style organization is a festival that looks the way the principal organizer wants it to look. If the organizer wants a family orientation, major events will be of interest to parents and children, the carnival will have lots of rides for younger children, and the beer garden will be given a low profile. Frequently, townspeople are willing to let the same organizer run the festival year after year. After all, having one person do all the work eases things for them considerably. The organizer feels that he or she is making a contribution to the community, which certainly is true; and members of the community know that if the organizer calls on them they, too, can contribute to the community in a way that is within their capacity. This form of control and continuity can produce excellent festivals.

But family-style organization is not without its hazards. The first is burnout. After a few years, the organizer may be exhausted. The job gets too routine or too overwhelming, the rewards are too slim, and the organizer concludes that it is time to pay attention to other things in life. Burnout is a serious problem, and not just personally for the organizer. After five, ten, or fifteen years as the festival's organizer, a person may appear to be the festival's owner. If the organizer decides to quit, the festival's continued existence is threatened, since no one else in the community has the same breadth of experience or involvement as the current festival organizer. Most people feel unable to devote the next ten or more years of their lives to the festival. If the principal organizer does not realize that he or she is burned out, of course, the festival begins to decline. The same old events are less and less vibrant, attendance drops, and the community's sense of attachment to the festival begins to evaporate.

The second danger with family-style festival organization is the possibility that people in the community may become increasingly alienated from the festival. After all, the community and the festival organizer are not one and the same. As long as the festival that the organizer delivers meets the approval of most segments of the community, things are fine. But it is always possible that some groups in the community will begin to feel excluded from the festival organized in their name. At that point, conflict surfaces. Small towns do change, after all. Members of the community grow up and move away. New people move in. There are more—or fewer—young children than there were before. A generation ages and its interests change. The festival has to make some concessions to the community it serves, and this may be difficult for a principal organizer who is comfortable doing the same things the same way year after year.

Corporate-Style Organization

The second form of festival organization is corporate. That is, the festival becomes a legal institution with a board of directors, a festival cabinet, and formal committees charged with organizing different aspects of the festival. One of the most elegant and effective examples of corporate festival organization is found in Glenwood. The Glenwood Waterama, established in 1956, has become one of the largest water festivals in the state outside the Minneapolis Aquatennial. It attracts visitors from all over Minnesota as well as from Iowa, Wisconsin, and the Dakotas. Waterama is incorporated, and the name is a registered trademark.

Waterama is organized on two levels. The upper level is made up of three men: the admiral at the top, followed by the commodore and the vice-commodore. The admiral oversees all the work on the festival and travels regularly during the spring and summer to other festivals throughout the state to promote Waterama. He is responsible for developing enthusiasm among the many people who work on the festival, and he gives each year's festival a particular tone. He also is responsible for grooming his successor, the commodore, whom he had chosen to serve with him two years earlier, back when he moved up from vice-commodore to commodore. In this way, the admirals form a chain of friends and business associates begun in 1956 and continued without break since then.

This same pattern of three-year terms of service, which has been at the heart of the success of Waterama, is repeated in the lower level of festival organization. Each aspect of the festival, from publicity to parade to queen pageant, has a committee. Each committee is made up of three couples, with each year's most recent members choosing another couple to join the committee for the next year. Six people make the work go much more easily. When the couples are friends, they can combine business with pleasure, meeting once a month to have supper together and work on details of their event. Most important, everyone involved in the festival recognizes that, whereas they have to serve for three years, each year will be different, and they need not serve more than three years if they do not want to. Of course, people who come to love the festival and want to stay involved can always find other committees that need help. The important point is that people see that they do not have to dedicate their lives to Waterama and that the community recognizes three years as reasonable service.

This form of organization is valuable in communities where business and professional people feel the need to involve themselves in community service, especially if there are a lot of new people moving into the business and professional parts of the community. Work on the festival provides both new and established people with an excellent means of contributing to the town; the festival is clean, family-oriented entertainment for lots of people and provides high visibility for its organizers.

Glenwood has undergone a good deal of population movement and commercial turnover since World War II. The organization of Waterama rapidly and effectively integrates people whose roots and ties are somewhere else. It speedily places new residents in contact with established members of the business and professional communities. Waterama requires intensive community service that creates ties between members of a geographically mobile middle class. It is the one aspect of life in Glenwood that defines the town; in an important way, Waterama *is* Glenwood, and Glenwood is Waterama. For the past forty years, Waterama has endured in Glenwood, whereas many people and businesses have come and gone. As a festival organizer in Montgomery remarked about his own festival (and it is as true for Glenwood), "Without Kolacky Days, what would Montgomery be? Just like a million other places."

While not every town's festival is as smoothly organized as the Glenwood Waterama, the corporate form of organization is widespread and effective. It provides newcomers to the business community with the opportunity to prove that they care about and are dedicated to their new town. After all, what more effective and visible way to demonstrate that you have committed yourself to living in your new town than to become involved with the community celebration? Corporate festival organization also makes the lines of local communication and decision making clear. The organization of play in these communities comes to reflect the organization of the world of work.

Indeed, many people who organize festivals claim that putting on a festival is a way for the businesspeople to "give something back" to the local community. They have made money from the people of the town and the surrounding areas all year long, and to do so without any return would be improper. It would be too distant, too grasping, too unneighborly. As one person explained, people who spend their money at local businesses all year long can become resentful if there is no sign that the business is putting something back into the community. Besides, the rise of regional shopping centers has made it even more necessary for local business owners to highlight their membership in, and dedication to, the community. For example, in St. Cloud, the owners of giant building-center stores (where things are cheaper and the selection better than the hardware stores or lumberyards in the small towns nearby) do not even live in St. Cloud, let alone in the small towns. The big building-center stores will not donate lumber for the counters at the beer tent. The local lumberyard owner might.

Giving something back to the community has long been a valid justification for getting involved in festivals. In 1935, the *Ortonville Independent* published an advertisement for the Northwestern State Bank of Ortonville, in which the bank invited everyone to the fifth annual Sweet Corn Festival, an event that had begun with the public donation of sweet corn by the new packing plant in town. "The day is one set aside for entertainment of folks from the countryside and everything is entirely free as a treat from Ortonville business firms—in a small measure one in appreciation of the patronage you have shown Ortonville in the past year."

In many communities following a corporate form of festival organization, to insure that the new people involved have a good sense of what needs to be done, notebooks are handed down from one event chairperson to the next. These notebooks always include a schedule for putting the event together, copies of letters that need to be sent out, people to contact, things to buy, and, often, notes on each year by each chairperson. These are very valuable aids in putting the event together.

In 1982, the Montgomery Jayceettes, now the Minnesota Women of Today, put together a notebook for the Kolacky Days queen pageant and kiddie parade that won them an award from the national organization of Jayceettes. The notebook, which includes a few pages of materials necessary for submission to the national organization, is twenty-eight pages long. It has sections detailing committee positions and areas of responsibility; a schedule of planning meetings; lists, by committee position, of materials needed; and an implementation schedule that begins six months in advance and runs through one week after the pageant. It is an excellent example of the kinds of materials that are included in guidebooks and that are necessary if corporate organization of a festival is to succeed.

The Montgomery women divided work for the pageant and kiddie parade into six subcommittees under a general chairperson: registration, buttons, judging, food, pageant, and kiddie parade. The level of detail in the notebook for the chair of each subcommittee is impressive. In the section on committee position and area of responsibility, for example, the subchairpeople for the pageant are to order crowns, plaques, and gifts for the candidates; plan and decorate for the pageant; contact the master of ceremonies, the lighting and sound person, escorts, and someone to provide music; prepare newspaper writeups on the candidates; write questions for each candidate to be asked at the pageant; and handle publicity for the pageant.

For materials, the guide indicates that the pageant subcommittee needs: 30 dolls (dolls are dressed in Bohemian costume, in keeping with the festival's theme, and are gifts for candidates and others connected with queen pageant); 1 organ; 3 crowns; 1 plaque; 1 platform; lights and sound; 2 ushers; decorations; 3 wicker chairs; 2 wicker tables; 2 Winnebago campers (used to transport candidates and as dressing rooms and "backstage area" outside the ball field where the pageant takes place); 1 robe; 1 sign; 1 drop cloth; 800 programs; 1 skirt for the platform; 50 note cards; 1 can of spray paint; 4 cars; stage props; 95 chairs; 4 tables; 1 easel; 1 podium; and 2 sets of bleachers.

Finally, the schedule to implement the pageant is lengthy and detailed. It is worth quoting directly here, because it gives as clear a picture as can be provided of the organization required for a successful festival, as well as the amount of help that is required.

6 MONTHS PRIOR
1. Order dolls from LTD Company—specify "no substitutes." The Germany dolls are ordered.

4 MONTHS PRIOR
1. Decide on music—if organ is used contact ———
2. Order crowns at David's Jewelry—one large and two smaller
3. Order plaque for Miss Congeniality
4. Decide if pageant will be held outdoors

3 MONTHS PRIOR
1. Contact Montgomery Public School—reserve from Wednesday through Saturday for pageant events
2. Ask for the janitors' assistance during this time as needed to help set up
3. Contact ——— in regard to lighting and sound for pageant and talent
4. Choose and contact M.C.—someone from the community
5. Plan decorations—if prom decorations are decided upon, contact ———
    —make plans to store decorations following prom until pageant if these are used
6. Contact ——— for chairs and tables
7. Arrange for Winnebagos to transport girls to park if pageant is held there and for judges to confer in to select the winners
8. Contact Williams Photography to attend pageant to take the pictures

2 MONTHS PRIOR
1. Contact ——— in regard to setting up the platform
2. Contact 2 junior boys for ushers—to attend talent judging and pageant
3. Contact Community Club President to do introduction and welcome at pageant

6 WEEKS PRIOR
1. Attend Salad Supper to talk to candidates about details of pageant
2. Get letters and pictures from Registration Chairmen

1 MONTH PRIOR
1. Do write ups of each candidate for the Montgomery Messenger using
   their resume
2. Divide write ups into three groups for use in the paper three weeks prior to
   the pageant
3. Article for Montgomery Messenger about the pageant
   —Time and place
   —Admission—Button & $1.00 or $2.00 without
4. Plan questions—take questions from their resume as much as possible so it
   is personal
5. Check about cleaning the robe
6. Contact reigning Queen about assisting the MC at the pageant
7. Contact the Queen and Princesses about rehearsal
8. Contact ———, MC, Community Club President, Mrs. ———, Lighting &
   Sound, Ushers and Janitors with a note to describe their duties
9. If pageant is indoors check into floor fans at U.S. Steel
10. Meet with MC to go over his duties
11. Get sign—have number changed
12. Get drop cloth from Jaycee Women closet
13. Black out Germany on doll boxes and gift wrap

2 WEEKS PRIOR
1. Line up Jaycee Women to help
2. Day of Florian [School of Cosmetology, in Minneapolis] visit inform candidates
   about rehearsal
3. Get traveling plaque from Queen
4. Call Bakery to check about using window for display
5. Put up display window—include:
   —dolls
   —plaques
   —crowns
   —sample of buttons
   —picture of reigning Queen
   —robe

6. Check with Community Club about skirt for platform
7. Decide on number of talent performers to have at the pageant—notify judging chairmen
8. Contact ———— to design program cover
9. Type inside of program
10. Take programs to school for printing
11. Contact MC, Community Club President, Ushers, Reigning Royalty to be at rehearsal
12. Type out MC cards—use the candidates' write ups from the paper
13. Contact reigning royalty for a short resume to use for their write ups
14. Take a note to janitors with specific needs

2 DAYS PRIOR
1. Set up platform
2. Have janitors move the bleachers

1 DAY PRIOR
1. Take down bakery window
2. Rehearsal—go over entire pageant with MC, ushers, candidates and Community Club President
3. Remind girls of hints they learned at Florian's
4. Go over procedure of entering, receiving rose at beginning, introducing parents, what to do with rose during questioning, where to walk for question, the recessional and receiving of doll as gift
5. Remind girls to bring clothes to school before 1:00 p.m. for the pageant on the day of the pageant
6. Handout "Candidates Instructions for Friday" sheet
7. Go through duties of new royalty for the week end:
   —attending the Kiddie Parade
   —parade on Sunday
   —grandstand on Sunday
   —softball tournament
8. Remind all candidates that they will be riding in the parade

DAY OF PAGEANT
1. Set up stage decorations, podium chairs
2. Have janitors bring chairs and needed items from school
3. Put skirt on platform
4. Mark grass with spray paint to mark where girls are to walk
5. Help ———— move organ to park
6. Lighting and sound will be set up after talent judging toward pageant time
7. Be at golf club about 4:30
8. Write up resume for introduction of judges
9. Write up resume for introduction of talent winners

10. Get envelope with Miss Congeniality [winner] from Judging
11. After supper is served take candidates to school to dress for pageant
12. Divide girls into two groups to ride to park in Winnebagos
13. Pageant—7:30
14. Have parents meet in designated area prior to pageant
15. Escort parents in just prior to pageant
16. Hold Monte Buck drawing during pageant
17. Have new Queen and Princesses and parents of Queen stay for pictures
18. Dismantle stage and return everything used

1 WEEK AFTER
1. Write thank you's
   —MC
   —Community Club President
   —Ushers
   —Janitors
   —Winnebago drivers
   —Organist
   —Past Queen for being MC
2. Submit bills to general chairman
3. Write report

Someone with little experience in working with a queen pageant would, with the help of this guide, be able to mount a successful event. And this, of course, is the wonderful thing about these detailed guides: the entire event (or festival, for that matter) does not have to be reinvented every year. Organizers can learn from the experiences of others, ensuring that there is consistency from year to year and that nothing important is omitted from the event.

But even this corporate form of organization has its drawbacks. Perhaps the most common hazard is the negative side of consistency: the dead hand of tradition. If the guidebooks begin to contain the entire festival, then problems emerge. The guidebooks should be exactly what they say they are—guides. Sometimes the individuals organizing an event are motivated more by a sense of duty than a love for the event. They follow the guidebook because they are not able to innovate or are not interested in innovating. Simply following the guidebook slavishly is as deadening as not following it at all.

There are other drawbacks as well. Finding volunteers has become the major challenge facing those responsible for corporately organized festivals. When volunteers are few, an enormous burden falls on their shoulders and those of the organizers. They may become resentful or burn out. Or, if they think the festival is important, they may adopt more of the family style of organization.

Whose Festival Is It?

In most towns, the people who put on the festival are small-business people, downtown merchants, lawyers, bankers, and others in similar occupations. For them, putting on the festival has a social component. They get to spend time with friends and associates working on something that is not business, and at the same time, their activity sets them apart from the people who do not put on the festival. The festival organizers work together hard for months, and their reward is not only the satisfaction of having mounted a successful festival but public recognition for the job they have done, in the form of compliments, thanks, and credit for their work at various events.

Festival organizers also develop closer connections with other like-minded people. Most festivals have what I call a "festival within the festival" for the people who put on the festival—a party, a dinner, or some other event that is only for them and reinforces their sense of fellowship and distinctiveness. Some of these are casual down-home kinds of events, featuring a buffet of cold cuts, bread, a couple of salads from the grocery store, soda pop, coffee, and beer. Others are elaborate, held at supper clubs or country clubs, with a catered buffet, a barbecue, or snacks, and a selection of beverages. For this reason, the festival-organizing group may be seen by some residents as a clique.

Like most elements of life, this aspect of festivals is a two-edged sword. There is no question that the festival within the festival serves to bring the organizers closer together, to help build camaraderie, to encourage them to continue to dedicate time and effort, and to reward them for a job well done. However, by its very nature, it separates the organizers from those for whom they are organizing. It is inevitably, if not always intentionally, exclusionary. While it rewards certain people for their help, it is also sets them apart, perhaps reinforcing the view some of them may already have of their own distinctive qualities. The irony, of course, is that in putting on an event designed to build community, the organizers can actually accentuate the differences in the community, strengthening their own community at the expense of the larger community of the town.

Outsiders and Communities

One of the other ways in which festivals build community is, paradoxically, by welcoming people who are not from the community. Many, perhaps even most, of those who throng the streets and parks of a town having its festival do not live in the town. Although festival organizers are notorious for inflating their crowd counts, many festivals do, in fact, attract more than twice the population of the town for a festival event like the parade.

But how does this build community? In 1958, the editor of the *Pope County Tribune,* published in Glenwood, wrote:

> The way we see it, a celebration of this type has two main benefits: (1) it develops an "esprit" among the people of the community and gives them a sense of pride in community achievement; and (2) Waterama does more to promote the Glenwood community than any other event possibly could. People come here from North and South Dakota, Iowa and other midwestern states, they like the celebration and they tell their friends about it when they get home.

By bringing off a successful celebration enjoyed by townspeople and outsiders alike, the citizens of the town recognize themselves as a community capable of working together to produce an event that satisfies them as well as those outside their town community. By recognizing this achievement of the townspeople, outsiders also make the townspeople aware of themselves as a community. Like the cast and crew of a successful theatrical event, they are able to attract an audience and please them.

This achievement should not be minimized. It is not easy bringing off a successful festival, and people are not wrong to be proud of what they have accomplished. But it is an interesting kind of arithmetic here. A small group of people has organized the festival. A somewhat larger group has helped with the work required by each event. A much larger group has attended or participated in events. But the organizers claim the community for themselves; they take themselves to be the community. The "community achievement" that the *Pope County Tribune* lauded is the achievement of a small group of people who often are taken for (and sometimes even take themselves for) the entire community. This is no different, really, from the way in which the queen pageant operates, substituting one small set of young women for the entire set of young people in the community. Indeed, this is the issue of representation. To what extent do the queen pageant candidates *represent* the young people of the community, and to what extent do the organizers of the festival *represent* the entire community? To the extent that they do, their claim of the community is unproblematic. But when they are not representative of the wider community, problems can result. Contention can emerge and resentments can build. Festivals are not always completely positive, happy, open, warm community builders. They can be, of course, and frequently are. But in a community with bitter factions, or in a community where distinctions between groups are at all pronounced, a festival can serve as an all-too-public symbol of dissension and inequality.

But I do not want to leave this discussion of putting on a festival in quite this way. I want to recall the first festival I studied in 1981. It was Wednesday night, the last night of Foley Fun Days. The huge parade, featuring most of the major competition high school bands in Minnesota, was over. The turnout had been immense. The carnival was crowded, and the beer wagon was doing land-office business—all twelve taps were in action, and as fast as pitchers were filled, they were sold. The streets teemed with people obviously enjoying themselves and each other. I was sitting in the apartment behind the florist's shop. Thelma Otto, the florist and longtime organizer of Foley Fun Days, had invited my students and me to join her and the people who had helped her organize the festival for a little supper. As I ate a sandwich, I thought about the two weeks we had spent in Foley before and during the festival. I thought about the remarkable amount of time, beginning in January, that Mrs. Otto had spent on planning the festival, the remarkable number of details she had kept in her head, and the unbounded enthusiasm she had maintained for the festival. I thought about the other people who worked with her, busy with their events and checking in with her regularly. I remembered the warm applause the audience at the queen pageant had reserved for her when she came up to remind them of the other events of the festival.

Sitting there in her living room as friends wandered in to comment on how well things had gone, to grab a bite to eat, to thank her, to sit quietly and enjoy having done a good job, I saw both the tiredness and the pleasure. Despite their evident exhaustion, there was a sense that although problems and disorder had threatened, Foley Fun Days had again been a success. The community had gathered together and celebrated. The conversation, up until then, had touched on how things had gone that year. By the time we left, they were talking about 1982.

Kolacky Days, Montgomery.

Kolacky Days, Mongomery.

Sinclair Lewis Days, Sauk Centre.

Kolacky Days, Montgomery.

"Crazy Days" sales. Flower Fest, St. Charles.

Kolacky Days, Montgomery.

Kolacky Days, Montgomery.

Kolacky Days, Montgomery.

Corn Fest, Ortonville.

Rutabagas for sale. Rutabaga Festival, Askov.

Rutabaga Festival, Askov.

Kolacky Days, Montgomery.

Bingo. Rutabaga Festival, Askov.

Cake walk. Rutabaga Festival, Askov.

orn Carnival, Cokato.

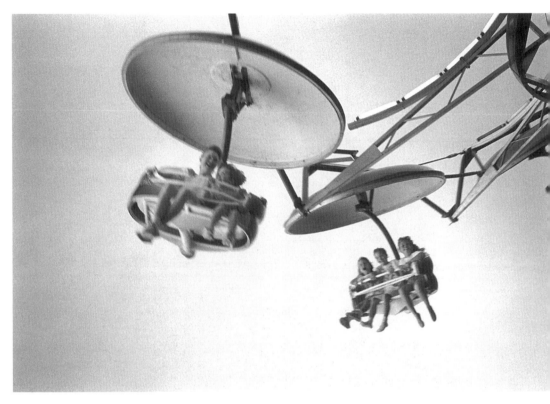

Corn Carnival, Cokato.

blacky Days, Montgomery.

Corn Carnival, Cokato.

Corn Carnival, Cokato.

Corn Carnival, Cokato.

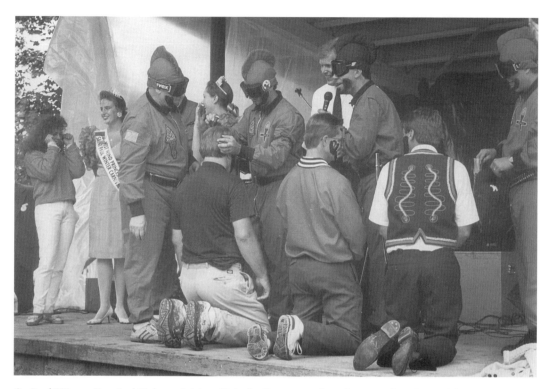

St. Paul Winter Carnival Vulcans initiate Kolacky Days organizers by smearing them with greasepaint at ceremony in park. Kolacky Days, Montgomery.

Volunteer helping with 10-K race finishers. Kolacky Days, Montgomery.

Queen pageant organizer with festival coordinator. Corn Carnival, Cokato.

Corn Fest, Ortonville.

St. Paul Winter Carnival Vulcans prepare to replenish the greasepaint on their faces before finding another woman who will agree to be smeared. Kolacky Days, Montgomery.

Prince of the East Wind, St. Paul Winter Carnival. Pola-Czesky Days, Silver Lake.

8. IN THE DEAD OF WINTER

In striking contrast to the small community festivals that have been my main subject thus far is the St. Paul Winter Carnival. It shares a number of features with festivals in small communities, including the creation of a culture of memory, marking the stages of life, building community, creating environments for having fun, and an organization dedicated to putting it on. But there are a number of significant differences between Winter Carnival and the small-town festivals. Some of the differences are found in elements present either in Winter Carnival or in the community festivals but not in both. Other differences are found in elements that are present in both but that take on different forms in each. Both sorts of differences throw into relief many of the features of the small-town festival. Several key features of the festivals of smaller communities are even more highly developed in the St. Paul Winter Carnival. The major differences derive from the differences between the size, complexity, and social organization of St. Paul and of small communities. Class divisions in St. Paul, in particular, are well established, multiply determined, and clear-cut. The ideology that everyone in town is fundamentally equal—an ideology that still has the power to make some people uncomfortable in medium-sized cities, where social divisions are sharper—has become little more than a slogan for many in St. Paul. This situation accentuates the prominence of certain features of the festival that have a lower profile elsewhere.

St. Paul, the capital of Minnesota, has a population of about 270,000, and is part of the Twin Cities metropolitan area of more than 2 million people. The

St. Paul Winter Carnival was celebrated irregularly in its early history, first in 1886, once again in 1916, and then again in 1936, before being celebrated yearly from 1946 to the present day. It is a large and elaborate undertaking that extends over twelve days in late January and early February. Winter Carnival boasts a full-time professional staff of four and a legion of over sixteen hundred volunteers. The carnival described herein took place in 1990, although it should be noted that a number of important changes occurred in 1992 as a result of a financial crisis precipitated both by unexpected expenses related to the extraordinary ice palace built in that Super Bowl year and by less commercial support than had been promised.

The St. Paul Winter Carnival operates on two levels, one of performance and one of administration and organization. The St. Paul Festival and Heritage Foundation (called the St. Paul Winter Carnival Association prior to 1992) is the body responsible for the official program of the event. Composed of a board of directors, a festival cabinet, and an executive director and three-member professional staff, it handles thematic coordination, fund-raising, publicity, and the scheduling of official Winter Carnival events. This is a year-round job, much of it behind the scenes for that reason. It is much more complex than the organization of community festivals, and highly corporate in nature.

For most residents of St. Paul, however, the distinctive features of Winter Carnival are to be found in performance, something almost totally lacking in other festivals. The Royal Family and the Vulcans, two uniformed groups, enact the fifty-year-old Winter Carnival legend during the last ten days of Winter Carnival and then travel all over Minnesota and beyond during the rest of the year. The Royal Family is composed of twenty-one members: King Boreas, who is King of Winter and the ruler of Winter Carnival; his brothers the Princes of the Winds—North, South, East, and West; the Queen of the Snows; the four Wind Princesses; the Prime Minister; the Captain of the Guard; and the nine King's Guards. The Royal Family makes over 150 appearances during the ten days, some public, some at Winter Carnival functions, many at hospitals, schools, nursing homes, and other care facilities.

Opposing these rather stodgy guardians of winter and social order are the eight Vulcans and Vulcanus Rex, the Fire King. The Vulcans dress in red running suits and capes, crested hoods, and ski goggles, and they smear black greasepaint on their cheeks and chin. Renowned in St. Paul for their traditional practice of kissing women and smudging them with greasepaint, the sooty symbol of the increasing power of the forces of warmth, the Vulcans now are permitted only to rub their faces against the cheeks of consenting women. The Vulcans are completely anonymous, both to the public and, publicly, to one another. During the festival, they refer to each other by their Vulcan names, such as the Prince of Ashes, Grand Duke Fertilious, or Baron Sparkus ("Sparky"). The Vulcans are the most carnivalesque feature of Winter Carnival. They lodge together during the ten days they are active in the festival, ride about the city in an antique fire truck, and make fun of the Royal Family and engage in mock battles with them.

Safe in their anonymity, the Vulcans, representing warmth and disorder, undermine the stuffed-shirt pomposity of the Royal Family and, by extension, the order they represent. At the end of every Winter Carnival, they make one final attack on the Royal Family, and win. Winter has been defeated. The Vulcans are the popular favorites, universally recognized and cheered throughout the city. Two of the students who worked with me in studying Winter Carnival had a chance to ride with the 1990 Vulcan Krewe on their fire truck for a few hours as they traveled to schools, nursing homes, hospitals, restaurants, and department stores. They reported that wherever in St. Paul they were—and they went through many of the city's neighborhoods—people honked their horns and waved, made the "V for Vulcan" sign, and shouted "Hail the Vulc!" As with everything carnivalesque, however, the Vulcans are not just safely domesticated figures of fun; they can be frightening and potentially dangerous. At night, leaping off the truck, capes flying, the powerful smell of alcohol enveloping them, running after women to smudge them even if the women object, they exude a whiff of the chaos that lies at the heart of carnivalesque disorder.

These uniformed groups are not officially part of the St. Paul Festival and Heritage Foundation. Each uniformed segment has its own alumni association, a fraternal order dedicated to choosing (sometimes) and supporting (always) the annual incumbents in the various roles. There are four Wind organizations, the Order of the Royal Guard, the Star of Boreas, the Queens, the Churchill Club (for former Prime Ministers), and most powerful, wealthiest, and best organized of all, Fire and Brimstone (for former Vulcans). There has also been a Women's Division, which has been the backbone of Winter Carnival and has seemed to be composed largely of wives of members of the uniformed groups, especially Fire and Brimstone. The Women's Division is now becoming a group open to men and women, to be called the Ambassadors.

Each fraternal order has its own uniforms for different occasions and produces emblems in the form of buttons, embroidered patches, pins—some to sell, some to distribute to other uniformed groups or to the public, and some with which to adorn themselves. These groups are active throughout the year, but their level of social activities increases near the time of Winter Carnival. Many of the events they sponsor, dinners especially, are officially open to anyone willing to buy tickets. These dinners are expensive; several informants remarked that it could cost about one thousand dollars per couple to attend all of them. For example, the October fund-raiser, called the Snow Ball, costs one hundred dollars per person, and about five hundred people usually attend. The dinner that precedes the royal coronation, which features the introduction and investiture of the new male members of the Royal Family and the coronation of the new Queen of the Snows and princesses, costs $50 per person. Slightly over one thousand people attended in 1990.

The jewelry, furs, clothing, hairstyles, cars, and deep tans on display at these events signal clearly that Winter Carnival is organized and performed by an elite. It takes money and position to be part of the core of Winter Carnival. All the members of the uniformed groups must be able to be absent from their jobs for ten days during the festival and must have the freedom afterward to make appearances on evenings and weekends (King Boreas and the Queen of the Snows now make over four hundred appearances a year). The King's Guards are men in their middle to late twenties who can afford the fifteen hundred dollars in uniforms, pins, lodging, food, and entertainment it will cost for the year. Vulcans are older and better established; it costs about three thousand dollars for a year in the krewe. Vulcanus Rex, usually in his forties or early fifties, generally spends about fifteen thousand dollars. The Prime Minister, usually a man in his early to middle thirties, spends about ten thousand dollars. The Princes of the Wind are usually in their forties and are well-known, successful businessmen chosen by their Wind organizations. It costs at least ten thousand dollars to be a Wind. Boreas must be a man at the height of an executive career, in his late forties or early fifties, who is prepared to make an investment upward of forty thousand dollars. Frequently, the corporations for which these men work contribute to their support, sometimes substantially. (For Boreas and Vulcanus Rex, the major expenses tend to be formal dinners for their supporters, which they underwrite. There are also expenses associated with travel. Boreas is expected to pay for some of the expenses of his court, especially the Queen of the Snows, when they are on the road. He also invests in several other items, including commemorative medals, coins, certificates, and three uniforms.)

During Winter Carnival, the major players, including the chairman of the board and the president of the festival cabinet, the chaperones for the queen and princesses, and all the uniformed characters, take up residence in three hotels in downtown St. Paul. One of these, the stately St. Paul Hotel, becomes the de facto center of the festival within the festival. Like the festival organizers in some medium-sized towns, the St. Paul elite regularly congratulates itself for its festival activities, although it does so in a rather more spectacular style. The festival within the festival that is concealed and almost furtive in smaller towns is openly, elaborately, vigorously, and joyously celebrated in St. Paul. As the doorman of the St. Paul Hotel remarked, "Those people know how to party."

For the people most deeply involved, the two weeks of Winter Carnival are a time of intense social activity. Those in a given year's performance wing (the uniformed groups that enact the carnival story) are suspended outside normal time and space in a "betwixt and between" state that the anthropologist Victor Turner called *liminal* (from the Latin word for threshold). They are separated physically, emotionally, mentally, and in attire and activity from their everyday lives. They live what appears to most of them later to have been a dream of remarkable power and affect. For those who put on the festival, there are parties, meetings, and events to attend and direct, and more parties. Those who are members of the fraternal organizations seem to participate in a round of parties and events that never stops. A former Vulcan reviewed his schedule for one of the weeks with me. Every night was taken up with some Winter Carnival–related social activity: the 7th St. Parade, a traditional Vulcan event that entails drinking in every bar along a street famous for the number of its bars; the reunion of Fire and Brimstone at the hotel to initiate and swear in the new krewe the night before the Vulcan Coming Out (an event for which my informant checked into the hotel to avoid the temptation to drive home and risk a DWI arrest); the reunion of his krewe (an event with wives); the get-together that his krewe always has with their successors; the Vulcan Conclave, the Fire and Brimstone business meeting; a party for the parade street directors (he was the director for parades); the West Wind dinner; and the Torchlight Parade and Vulcan Victory Dance. While this man's schedule may have been a bit more crowded than most, my students and I regularly saw the same faces at the social events associated with Winter Carnival that we attended (by no means all of them).

This festival within the festival reflects, perhaps, the intensity of the experiences of those who have performed in Winter Carnival. They have created a social world that they find compelling and satisfying, and that extends beyond the specifics of Winter Carnival. They patronize one another's businesses; they vacation with one another; they marry one another; they have their own language of address and reference. They even have their own kinship system—for example, the Princes of the Winds are brothers to Boreas, and men who have had the same Vulcan name in different years have been heard to refer to each other as "brother"—and a lengthy formal protocol manual. Indeed, the president of the festival cabinet, a senior vice president at the St. Paul Companies, told me his response to friends who were asking why anthropologists were studying Winter Carnival was, "We've created a culture here, with tribal differences and so on, and that's something anthropologists study."

The public performance itself, however, plays with symbols of domination and appropriation. The strongly emphasized, hierarchical royalty provides one field for the expression of these symbols. The Royal Family dresses in elaborate costumes that proclaim and catalogue hierarchy. In a given year, the Princes of the Winds might appear as an oriental potentate, a Mexican upper-class charro, a vaguely tartar lord, and a wealthy cowboy in leather coat, silver buckle, and snakeskin boots. The Prime Minister and King Boreas wear the kinds of military uniforms worn by modern European royalty, the king with a scepter; the queen and princesses wear formal attire with crowns; and the King's Guards wear military uniforms with braid. The language of subjects and rulers ("our right royal city"); the knightings of worthy people (even anthropologists, who become Royal Researchers) into the service of Boreas; the medals bestowed and buttons distributed; the captain of the King's Guards with his sword; and the guards themselves, who march in a distinctive rhythmic step into every public setting—all provide an overwhelming image of political domination. The Landmark Center—the old federal courts building in St. Paul, now beautifully restored and a symbol of the city—becomes the King's Castle. In its three-story atrium, carnival workers erect a dais with two thrones, one for King Boreas and one for the Queen of the Snows. The Grande Day and Torchlight Parades are the most popular Winter Carnival events in those years when an ice palace is not constructed, and they are televised statewide. These parades are filled with floats carrying the Royal Family and members of the different fraternal orders. Most St. Paulites know that the members of the uniformed groups are wealthy, and they see that almost all the players are male and all are white. Here is an elite with very clear criteria for membership. Their festival performance suggests that they deserve this position, and they are not shy about advertising and celebrating the rightness of their dominion.

The Royal Family, in particular, has appropriated the right to speak for St. Paul. In speech after speech, King Boreas talks about the pleasure and honor of representing Winter Carnival *and* the city of St. Paul. In the promotional material, too, the same conflation is made. When the Royal Family travels to Winnipeg; Austin, Texas; Bradenton, Florida; Memphis, Tennessee; or to small towns throughout the state, its members see themselves, and are referred to by their hosts, as representing not just St. Paul Winter Carnival but St. Paul itself. This, in the context of present-day St. Paul, is problematic. The community ethos of St. Paul is one of pluralism, or at least involves an ideology of multiple communities and distinct neighborhoods. The celebration of domination and the claim of representativeness are contradicted both by the official ideology of the city and the everyday experience of its citizens. Among those aware of this contradiction, many belong to groups that do not see themselves in Winter Carnival. They, and others, reject or ignore details of Winter Carnival that are most important to the insiders. For example, the attendance by the general public at the coronation has been declining over the past few years; in 1990 there were fewer people in the free-admission balcony seats than on the main floor at the fifty-dollar-per-person tables. Instead, the general public has concentrated on those events that are urban entertainments—the snow-sculpture and ice-carving contests, the firebird and Orthodox chapel created by the Soviet ice carvers, and the parades. Note that although the celebration of domination is problematic, it still happens. The covert move to impute universality to the interests of a small, elite group in smaller towns is much more overt here.

But excluded citizens in St. Paul expressed much less resentment to us than we encountered in some other, medium-sized towns. In part, I believe, this is because the Vulcans represent an ironic counter to the Royal Family. The ordinary people of St. Paul can support the Vulcans, cheering them on as they poke fun at the Royal Family and sow a little disorder. It does not seem to matter that the Vulcans hardly differ from the Royal Family in background: white, male, wealthy, on the way up. (Perhaps the only difference is that the only Jews in Winter Carnival have been Vulcans.) The resentment that people might feel toward the festival's organizers is deflected, although not erased, by the Vulcans. Further, the show put on in St. Paul is better than the show put on elsewhere, and for obvious reasons. The entire budget for the Hutchinson Water Carnival, a good-sized festival in a city of over nine thousand, is the budget for one Winter Carnival parade in St. Paul. The scale of the organizations is hardly comparable; for example, the organizers of the St. Paul Winter Carnival arranged to bring in ice carvers from the USSR in 1990 and from China in 1989. The St. Paul Winter Carnival also offers a wider range of events for different constituencies, from ski and snowshoe races and hockey tournaments to concerts, parades, dances, children's events, senior-citizen events, and an indoor fair with midway, music, craft sales, concessions, displays, and more.

Nevertheless, as in medium-sized and small towns, the organizers of Winter Carnival do not speak with one voice. The executive director in 1990, a remarkable man named Robert Carter Jr., as centrally located within the Winter Carnival organization as it is possible to be, was keenly aware of many of the contradictions of Winter Carnival. He worked on strategies to do something about them without alienating the core of Winter Carnival people who have devoted an enormous amount of time and money to the festival and who have built their social lives around it. For example, following the 1990 coronation, he decided that the following year the princesses would no longer kneel in front of their Wind Princes to receive their crowns. He also worked to change the image of the Queen of the Snows from that of a virginal daughter of the community to that of a major

St. Paul businesswoman, the female equivalent of King Boreas. Carter is aware
that some people in St. Paul believe that Winter Carnival is just a fraternity party
for rich white businessmen, and he hoped to change that image by decentralizing
the carnival, moving events into St. Paul's neighborhoods and inviting representatives of ethnic and racial groups to develop their own events under the carnival
rubric (a process that has continued since his departure). He is not alone in his as-
sessment of Winter Carnival, but he does not represent the only voice within carnival. There are many who like Winter Carnival just as it is, and some would quit
if the festival changed much at all. Carter himself recognized the multiple interpretations of Winter Carnival. He pointed out, in regard to his proposal to make
the Queen of the Snows a major businesswoman, that for every woman who felt
it was about time to make this change, there was at least one who swore that if it
happened she would never support Winter Carnival again.

The future of Winter Carnival is not, of course, something that the organizers
alone will decide. As in every other community, the future of the carnival will also
be shaped by the wider economic, political, and cultural changes going on in the
community and by the contested interpretations of these changes.

For example, distinct from organizers of small-town festivals and the Hutchinson Water Carnival, many, perhaps most, of the people involved in organizing and
performing in Winter Carnival are St. Paul natives. Growing up in the tradition,
sometimes with fathers or grandfathers who had been part of Winter Carnival,
many St. Paulites have come to see Winter Carnival as an important focus for
their own social and business activities. But the changes in the economic base of
St. Paul brought about by corporate restructuring and consolidation have had an
effect on Winter Carnival. Many formerly independent businesses have become
part of larger corporations, and some of the larger corporations have moved their
headquarters to Minneapolis or have moved large segments of their workforces
out of state. Of the three great St. Paul breweries that had been of signal impor-
tance to the festival over the years, Hamm's is gone, and the Stroh's and Schmidt
breweries were taken over by larger beer conglomerates. During the 1991 Winter
Carnival, the city of St. Paul had to begin seriously considering ways of keeping
the Stroh's and Schmidt breweries from closing, a task at which they were unsuccessful, although the Schmidt building is in use by a new, much smaller local
brewery.

The other side of the economic transformation is the development of "corporate suburbs" made up in large measure of people who have been transferred into
the St. Paul area. While these people are expected to become involved civically,
such localized civic activities as Winter Carnival may not be as attractive to them
as national activities like the United Way or the Heart Association, membership

in which is portable. Here is another challenge that Winter Carnival must face, and the strategies put in place now for attracting volunteers will shape the future of the festival.

The attempt to bring other ethnic groups and neighborhoods into the carnival may be understood in several ways. On one hand, it can be seen as a long-overdue recognition that Winter Carnival must work actively to be inclusive rather than exclusive, that its claim to represent all of St. Paul rings hollow without the participation of other constituencies. But on the other, it can be seen as conferring a kind of second-class citizenship on people who cannot afford to become part of the core group of Winter Carnival. It highlights the difficulty that Winter Carnival is having in finding people who can be seen as representative of these multiply voiced communities in St. Paul. It can also be interpreted as an attempt to extend middle-class control outward into ethnic and working-class communities, incorporating groups that already have their own ethnic festivals. But in diversifying the makeup of Winter Carnival, more volunteers are available, and Winter Carnival must respond to the changes in the corporate volunteer pool.

The growing litigiousness of American society has caused the Winter Carnival organizers to cancel, rethink, or replace several traditional, classic participatory Winter Carnival events, ranging from the ice palace (insurance companies would not write liability insurance except at an almost impossibly high cost; engineers and architects refused to "inspect" the construction, although they would "observe" it) to toboggan runs and ice slides for children. The effect of the loss or the scaling back of these events is felt in the public participation in Winter Carnival, which declines and is being replaced with increased spectatorship.

Winter Carnival is distinct among Minnesota festivals in having a powerful carnivalesque image at its heart. The size of the city, the complexity of the city's organization, the anonymity it offers, and its fundamental incomprehensibility—all make the carnivalesque activities of the Vulcans possible. But there have also been attempts since the late 1970s to control carnivalesque disorder by limiting what the Vulcans can do. There is a clear ambiguity in the figure of the Vulcan who represents freedom and challenges the domination of the "rulers" by attacking women. The simultaneous impacts of the women's movement and the rise of litigiousness have led the Vulcans to feel beleaguered and have forced them to clean up their act. They have modified many of their traditional practices; for example, they no longer kiss and smudge all women they can reach, many traditional pranks that they once directed toward the Royal Family are now directed to the incoming krewe, and they are trying to shift public attention to their civic activities. But the public still expects the Vulcans to be as the public remembers them. Winter Carnival is deep in people's memories and the history of St. Paul; the weight of that performance tradition also serves to control the performers. People would be disappointed if the Vulcans became too tame, however politically correct or legally prudent that might be. At the same time, many members of Fire and Brimstone oppose the women's movement, decry the litigiousness of modern American society, and resent the changes that have been implemented or suggested. Some Vulcans on the street push at the edges of the changes, for instance, smearing women even if they protest.

It should be clear, however, that the way Winter Carnival is manifest in the memories of St. Paulites is different than the way festivals appear in memories of those in small towns. Ample opportunities exist in St. Paul for people to connect their memories to events of Winter Carnival, but very few who attend Winter Carnival events know the other people there. To almost everyone who sees them, the uniformed group members are nothing more (or less) than the parts they play. Who they are in real life is neither known nor relevant. But in the small community, such is not the case; organizers are known by many of the people who participate in or enjoy the festival, and hence cannot really ever escape into their roles. There is always a certain transparency to public roles in a small town, as people are known in many different ways and through the many other roles they play. As well, many of the people at the festival know each other, and the festival itself is understood as a *community* festival. As a result, people's memories attach to the community as well as to the festival. In Winter Carnival, for people who are not members of the uniformed groups and their organizations, the site of memories is personalized and little different from the memories any regular urban entertainment might provoke. The uniformed groups and the Vulcans provide people with memories, as do ice palaces, of course, but the intimate connection between community and memory is attenuated.

The women's movement has also had an effect on the coronation ritual of the Royal Family. Formerly, the wives of the Princes of the Winds and Boreas were never even mentioned, let alone introduced, during this ceremony. Today, members of the uniformed groups in Winter Carnival now formally recognize the contributions of wives to the husbands' role activities. In 1990, the wives of both the outgoing and the incoming princes and Boreases even appeared on stage with their husbands. Let me take a moment to describe these scenes. Each outgoing fortyish prince and his princess in her early twenties came forward from the royal grouping at the back of the stage to receive recognition from the crowd. The prince's wife was then introduced and came onto the stage, joining her husband and his princess. She received a bouquet of roses from her husband, kissed him, and then leaned across him to embrace the princess. Together, all three, husband in the middle, acknowledged the cheers of the crowd. The incoming prince was then introduced and, with his wife, climbed the steps to the end of the runway, some twenty feet or more from the front of the stage. Husband and wife walked together about a third of the way to the stage, where they stopped and kissed. She returned to the steps and disappeared into the darkness. Her husband, the prince, continued forward to the stage, where a line of twenty young women, the contestants in the Queen of the Snows competition, waited. Moments later, he received his princess, who knelt before him to receive her crown from his hands.

To an anthropological observer, this ceremony looks like either a ritual of acceptance by a first wife of her husband's new wife in a polygynous society or, alternatively, the public bestowal of a subservient second (or "trophy") wife with at least the tacit approval of the senior wife. I do not want to suggest that the organizers wished to achieve this problematic, tension-producing, awkward outcome. Far from it. I do wish to point out, however, in traditional anthropological terms, how their good-faith attempts at change can produce unexpected results and how the serious pursuit of change in the role of women is bound to affect the structure of Winter Carnival at levels the organizers might not have anticipated. The modified coronation ceremony was, after all, designed to reflect positively the contemporary, egalitarian model of husband-wife relations and to recognize explicitly the wife's contribution. Yet it had quite the opposite effect, throwing into sharp relief the conflict, especially in the marriages of successful men, between duty to wife and attraction to an image of oneself as having earned the right to appear in public with a beautiful young woman on one's arm. The conflict was certainly present in the performance and was obvious to more observers than just the anthropologist.

Here, then, the power of the small-town queen pageant to highlight coming of age, to emphasize an egalitarian community ideology of achievement, and to symbolize the capacity of the community to produce outstanding young people is turned around. The Winter Carnival coronation is for an elite. People involved in the St. Paul business community may know, or have heard of, the various princes or King Boreas, but they are a distinct minority. Almost no one knows the candidates in the Queen of the Snows competition. To the observers, there is nothing more in the coronation except an enactment of the Winter Carnival story and the continuation of the "royal lines" of carnival. To the outsiders, the messages of the coronation are ambiguous. The clarity of the small-town pageant is gone; indeed, overall, the clarity of the small-town festival is gone. Winter Carnival is an urban entertainment as well as a festival, a spectacle in which the traces of the small-town festival are still to be seen, but one in which the commercial and personal interests characteristic of any major metropolitan area strongly shape the festival, emphasizing performance over participation.

Winter Carnival entertains the community and provides people with the material for creating their own personal memories. Unlike the small community festival, it does not present the community to itself, thereby providing a site for reunion and community memory.

AFTERWORD

Although this work is not intended as a scholarly monograph on festivals, I would like briefly to consider several issues of current anthropological concern that emerge in the text. I have concentrated on the public construction of both memory culture and the place of the individual in the collectivity. Although it is my contention that Minnesota festivals create a contested and contestable public culture, a field of political and cultural forces constituted by events satisfying different tastes and subject to the play of varying interests, festivals are distinctly accented by the nature of the communities in which they occur. For this reason Minnesota festivals are not all identical.

At the same time, although there are a great many festivals in Minnesota, the amount of variation is limited, partly because of the structural commonalities of local and regional integration. The processes of community building within the frame of the late-twentieth-century Minnesota state political economy present communities with similar problems to solve, and the solutions, though not always identical, resemble one another. The similarity is due in part to people's common experiences as members of American, Midwestern, and Minnesota culture and in part to the desire to dramatize some specific notions of personhood in communities. But the notions of personhood are self-negotiable. The distinction is perhaps most clearly drawn in the contrast between the corporate and family forms of organization, where the person as team player, able to work well with others, is juxtaposed to the person as independent worker—adult, entrepreneur, farmer. But even here the vision of the person as self-efficacious—"we work on the festival because we are supposed to"—is common to both versions. This idea of agency, which includes asserting the social and cultural potency of the person in a public context and requires acting in the creation of community, seems to lie at the heart of festival action.

However, the social ties in Minnesota communities are fragile and contingent. In the small towns, these ties must be nurtured and protected. In such communities, divisiveness is a danger to the community's survival as a more or less coherent entity. The people who remain in these communities earnestly support the communitarian ideology, avoiding the corrosive irony of carnival (see Lavenda 1988). This ideology is plausible and necessary because the town is small. A midsized Minnesota town—Hutchinson would be a good example—is sufficiently diverse and divided that the communitarian ideology is both implausible and less vital for the life of the city. This diversity and division lead to a split in the city that the festival makes plain.

In a large city like St. Paul, a monolithic communitarian ethos is both implausible and unachievable, and the festival's potential for making visible and "thinkable" the sharp divisions within the city is shaped and colored by the presence of the Vulcans. The Vulcans do not deny the divisions, they incarnate them. And because the dialogue is formalized in play, there are antagonisms but nobody gets hurt. Beyond that, King Boreas and the Vulcans form a necessary combination. Neither makes sense without the other, and the outcome of their struggle creates the image of a playing field that is truly level. After all, even though the Vulcans triumph at the end of Winter Carnival, by the next January, Boreas is back on his throne and the Vulcans must break out once again.

Abner Cohen (1980, 83) points out that "carnivals are irreducible cultural forms, but, like all other cultural forms, are seldom free of political significance. They range in their political functions from the maintenance of the established order, serving as 'rituals of rebellion,' to the articulation of protest, resistance and violence against that order. The same carnival may vary in its politics over time." I wish to suggest that they may speak with and to more than one voice at the same time and that, indeed, this loophole is the dialogic potential at the heart of public culture.

This loophole, however, is situated within a broader sense of order, that of social order, discussed by David Chaney (1993). His argument, that public dramas are inextricably embedded in the ideological constitution of social order—"the predictable, indeed, the prescribed, character of everyday life"—is particularly apt for the study of small-town festivals. As should be clear, even from the necessarily sketchy material presented here, festivals provide participants at every level of the social world with the opportunity to reflect on themselves as parts of a collectivity. Thus, masquerading as moments when everyday life is suspended, festivals are (to use Chaney's phrase) "a form of inscription in which different programmes of collective remembering and systematic forgetting can be enacted" (1993, 20). In essence, they are a part of the way in which the everyday is constructed in small towns. As a consequence, they are open to the various interpretations of different kinds of participants as well as to the normalization of structural differences in power between groups.

At the same time, the festival's very "normality," its cyclic and unthreateningly public quality, allows it to become a site where public and private memory conjoin, and it is from memory that culture forms. As a play form, the subjunctive quality of the community festival allows people the possibility of ignoring the festival, but it also allows the festival the possibility of taking on an unlooked for and unexpected significance in people's individual and communal lives. The play world and the not-play world leave residues—traces—in each other, and the shape of the play world is affected by the shape of the not-play world and vice-versa. Both worlds are in constant contact. As festivals satisfy, or do not satisfy, the people involved with them, they insinuate themselves into the quotidian through the sheer pleasure, or annoyance, they provoke. The opportunity that festivals as play forms provide players is the opportunity to decide to interpret the festival "for real" or "for play."

Festivals as institutions inhabit the borderland between play and not-play. The work of putting on a festival is still work, festival bills still need to be paid, liability insurance must be purchased, the parade route must be marked off, and traffic must be directed. And there are people who become involved in festivals not for the pure joy of play but to further their careers, make connections in the business community, prove their commitment to their new place of residence. Once the festival starts, the fluid boundary of play is crossed, and the social world of the town looks different, although recognizable. Indeed, it is precisely Georg Simmel's notions of sociation and sociability, "the play form of sociation," that are relevant here. The space of the festival would seem to be a space that is an end in itself, and of course, it is, or better stated, it may be. And no one could argue that the festival does not provide opportunities for sociability. As Simmel suggests (1950, 49), sociability exists for its own sake; it has no objective purpose and no extrinsic results. Peripheral aspects of the everyday world are transformed into the meaning of sociable situations. The world created in sociability, then, is a delicate one, and Simmel points out that the game becomes a lie when the play of sociability becomes harnessed to intentions and events of practical reality.

Because sociability is a play form, its frame is permeable, the line between sociability and such aspects of practical reality as sociation is ambiguous, and the exact whereabouts of that line is subject to interpretation and negotiation. Overall, then, what the previous chapters suggest is that, in the small town, the festival provides the opportunity for people to experience themselves as members of a community that transcends mere coresidence, and it provides an opportunity for agency for one set of people—the organizers—as they act *in* the community *as* community members. Indeed, it can be argued that attending the festival, to the degree that people must choose to attend, itself provides an environment for agency.

But the organization of the festival, and the experiences of festivalgoers, have consequences outside the festival, opening possible directions for interaction, social activity, and sociation that might not have been there before.

Hence, in the small town, the festival provides opportunities for living life in public and for recognizing the social construction of the self on a relatively broad basis. That this is not universally so is clear from the example of the St. Paul Winter Carnival, where people's festival experience of the self is a much more bounded one, limited to voluntary associations and, save for the uniformed participants, an absence of a sense of a personal connection to St. Paul. Indeed, the Winter Carnival differs from the small-town festival not just in terms of scale, but in an essential feature of its nature; Winter Carnival has become a *spectacular,* "a mode of performance in which possible experience is visualised in order to impress an audience" (Chaney 1993, 22). It implies an audience, spectators rather than participants, whose connection to the collectivity need not be anything more than tenuous. Winter Carnival is sociable and celebratory, and it is a site for memories, but St. Paul as a place does not become part of those memories except as a backdrop, nor does "St. Paul" understood as a moral community.

The history of small community festivals in Minnesota makes clear the contingent, local nature of festivals. While it may well be the case that celebration is a human universal, the particularities of celebration need to be considered ethnographically. Festivals in Minnesota communities ebb and flow, and the festival in any given town that appears to be as old as the town itself frequently turns out to have started in the 1970s or 1980s in response to specific local concerns. Even the St. Paul Winter Carnival, which actively promotes itself as having more than one hundred years of history, has been celebrated continuously only since 1946. The illusions of ancientness and traditionality are connected to the increasing sense that very few enduring configurations of communal identification reach beyond the familial, even in small towns. Eric Hobsbawm's influential discussion of "invented traditions" (see both his articles in Hobsbawm and Ranger, 1983) directs our attention both to the role of such traditions in establishing or symbolizing social cohesion, or the membership of groups, meaning real or artificial communities (Hobsbawm 1983a, 7–9), and to the absence of other forms of cohesion in the middle class (Hobsbawm 1983b, 303). Frank Manning (1983, 25–26), paraphrasing Dean MacCannell, writes: "[MacCannell] contends that modern cultural productions are centrally preoccupied with authenticity. As the modern world itself is seen as shallow and spurious, our most popular cultural productions (which, *inter alia,* are typically tourist attractions) are based on themes drawn from other cultures, or, more likely, from the historical past."

Yet the characteristic contempt of the modern and postmodern academic theorist for the culture of the small-town American middle class (see, for example, Dorst 1989 for a particularly egregious example) masks the fundamental issue at work: people who wish to live in communities need to engage in activities that establish a social order through which community life can be carried out. Given what David Chaney (1993, 194) calls the balkanization of identity, the creation and maintenance of any community requires work. Festivals in small Minnesota towns are part of this work.

Hence, the study of festivals in Minnesota is part of the study of the nature of communal life and the creation of means by which individuals connect themselves to wider groups. Small communities do not have to be "imagined communities," a phrase from Benedict Anderson (1983); they can be directly experienced through festival participation. That these festivals are voluntary and entertaining rather than obligatory and transformative—closer to the liminoid end of Turner's continuum than to the liminal—makes them no less important in the structuring of the sense of the community self. Indeed, I have argued in this work that given the nature of communities in middle-American life, more intense forms of establishing a communally connected self are impossible—there are too many other demands on the socially situated self. At some level, however, people seem to think there is a community life that must be sustained. The network of voluntary associations that characterize American life serves to direct interaction and structure relationships. The power of the festival is its capacity to entertain and to reach beyond the limits of organizations that require a stronger commitment or specialized knowledge or interests, such as families, professional groups, or hobby associations.

Celebration is connected with a wide range of other dimensions of a community's life—economic, political, social, religious. The study of celebratory activities, then, becomes the study of the community itself. It is at this point that ethnographic studies of particular festivals in particular communities become salient. As noted above, festivals, although similar, are not all identical; communities accent their festivals differently. While similarities in events and political organization are based on structural similarities in the communities involved—on the one hand, parades, queen pageants, dances; on the other, control by the small-town business community—the particular shape of the festival varies. This is especially true

in the way the festival represents the insertion of the community in the wider world of region and state—said insertion glossed sometimes as "modernity" (see Manning 1983). Some small festivals, the Glenwood Waterama of the early 1980s, for example, wholeheartedly embrace the increasing regionalization and outward direction of the Minnesota rural political economy, a system of educational, governmental, and medical consolidation, industrial parks, tourism, and regional integration. Waterama is a festival that, by its organizational structure, welcomes outsiders to enjoy the celebration and welcomes newcomers to the business community. Other small festivals—Foley Fun Days of the early 1980s is a good example—resist the same pressures. Foley Fun Days welcomed outsiders only for events at the beginning and end of the festival, but preserved the central festival events for the home community and concentrated the organization of the festival in the hands of a small number of people with long-term ties to the community. Nevertheless, as suggested above, the range of possible variation is narrow; people work with the materials at hand; there are no little towns that "time forgot, that the decades cannot improve," as Garrison Keillor says about his fictitious Lake Wobegon.

What makes American festivals anthropologically interesting, even compelling, is the same interplay of global elements and local concerns that anthropologists have found everywhere else they have done fieldwork. It is, after all, this interplay that makes communities both distinct and recognizable as part of a wider culture. Festivals, because they are public and because they are play, are an effective means of revealing the particularities of the inner lives of communities.

A NOTE ON SOURCES

Festivals

The scholarly literature on nonreligious festivals is not vast. Readers interested in overviews of the central issues can examine Alessandro Falassi's introductory essay (1987) and Roger Abrahams's essay (1987), both in *Time Out of Time: Essays on the Festival,* as well as Abrahams and Richard Bauman (1978), Robert J. Smith (1972), Beverly Stoeltje (1983), and Frank Manning's important essay (1983) on the festival.

General works on festivals that have shaped my thinking are Don Handelman's dense and theoretically sophisticated explorations of the structure of festivals and public events of various kinds (1992, and the works collected in Handelman 1990); Clifford Geertz's classic study of the Balinese cockfight (1972) as well as collections of his more general theoretical writings (1973 and 1983, especially "Religion as a Cultural System" in the former and "Art as a Cultural System" in the latter); Victor Turner's various writings on ritual and play (e.g., 1969, 1982, 1983); Mikhail Bakhtin's work on Carnival (1968); and David Cheney's recent and important work on spectacle and public drama (1995).

Other useful and important works on the theory of festivals include Ronald Grimes on public ritual in Santa Fe, New Mexico (1976); Denise L. Lawrence on the Doo Dah Parade in Pasadena, California (1987); James Fernandez on festivals in Asturias (1986); and Hans Buechler's magnificent study of the rural-urban festival system of Bolivia (1980). A theoretical study of anthropological writing that deals with issues of irony and the festive is by George Marcus and Michael Fischer (1986). One classic analysis of irony is by literary theorist Wayne Booth (1974).

Readers interested in the issues of memory and nostalgia discussed in chap. 1 may consider works by Jack Kugelmass (1992), Paul Connerton (1989), and Maurice Halbwachs (1980), though none specifically treat festivals. Two important studies of tradition and its connections with memory, nostalgia, and national identity directly relevant to the ways in which festivals portray the past are Eric Hobsbawm and Terence Ranger's well-known collection on the ways in which apparently ancient traditions have been invented (1983) and John Tomlinson's brilliant study of cultural imperialism (1991).

Small-Town Festivals

Here the scholarly literature is very thin. Of W. Lloyd Warner's multivolume study of "Yankee City" (Newburyport), Massachusetts, one, *The Living and the Dead: A Study of the Symbolic Life of Americans,* includes a long section on the Yankee City Tercentenary Parade (1959). Another classic ethnographic work from the 1950s is Ronald Frankenberg's study of soccer and community festivals in Wales (1957), a work especially important because it addresses how a succession of public events, one of which was a carnival, designed to build community in the town of "Pentradiwaith" failed as a result of internal disputes and feuds in the town. Frederick Errington has published two studies of festivals in "Rock Creek," Montana (1987, 1990) that address issues of irony, seriousness, and the ways in which solid middle-class citizens in the town can reflect on the wisdom of the life choices they have made by comparing themselves to the traveling rodeo cowboys. Marjorie R. Esman writes of the celebration of ethnic identity among Louisiana cajuns and the ritual release of tensions in the community that the festival permits (1982). Sheldon Smith has written about festivals and communities in Westby and La Crosse, Wisconsin (1984). Beverly Stoeltje has written extensively about cowboy festivals in west Texas towns (see especially 1987, 1988). The most extended study of a festival in a relatively small town is Richard Swiderski's book about San Pietro Festival in Gloucester, Massachusetts (1986), an only partially successful attempt to apply a Bakhtinian perspective to the study of festival behavior in the United States. Carole Farber has written a valuable study of a homecoming festival in Mt. Forest, Ontario, a small town with some demographic and cultural similarities to the Minnesota communities that form the basis for this book (1983). A photo-essay on midwestern fairs is Greta Pratt's *In Search of the Corn Queen* (1994), with an introductory essay by Karal Ann Marling.

Minnesota Culture and Small Towns

There are a number of valuable sources on Minnesota culture. The most famous are fictional: Sinclair Lewis's *Main Street* and *Babbitt* (the state in which Zenith is located is never specified in the novel, but it certainly reads like Minnesota), and Garrison Keillor's *Lake Wobegon Days* and *Leaving Home* (1985 and 1987, respectively). Other important works are by Karal Ann Marling, who has written extensively on Minnesota popular culture and who briefly visits small-town festivals in *The Colossus of Roads: Myth and Symbol along the American Highway* (1984) and "Culture and Leisure: The 'Good Life' in Minnesota" (1989).

Marling also has a very fine study of the Minnesota state fair (1990), an event that in its reunion, coming-of-age, and carnivalesque aspects has some resonance with community festivals, although it is quite distinct in terms of audience, structure, and atmosphere. The county fairs are an important counterweight to the community summer festivals, as discussed in chap. 4. Patrice Avon Marvin and Nicholas Curchin Vrooman provide a history of the Goodhue County Fair, with a section of comments by a variety of Goodhue County people about the modern fair at the end (1985). An excellent recent work on midwestern county fairs in Illinois and Wisconsin is Leslie Prosterman's *Ordinary Life, Festival Days: Aesthetics in the Midwestern County Fair* (1995). Prosterman is particularly interesting on the aesthetics of animal and product judging and its relation to the aesthetics of everyday life.

Perhaps the most important work on Minnesota folk culture is Willard B. Moore's introductory essay to the catalogue for the University of Minnesota Arts Museum's landmark show, "Circles of Tradition" (1989). Important material on folklife aspects of Minnesota culture is also to be found in *The Minnesota Ethnic Food Book* (Kaplan, Hoover, Moore 1986). From a social science perspective, Don Martindale and R. Galen Hanson's *Small Town and the Nation: The Conflict of Local and Translocal Forces*, a 1969 study of Benson, Minnesota, is an essential resource. Hervé Varenne's ethnographic study about Wisconsin (1977) is a very important source for anyone interested in the midwestern small town. Essays by Thomas Harvey on small-town Minnesota and by David L. Nass on the rural experience (both 1989) are important overviews of the history and contemporary situation in their respective areas.

Carnival

A number of important works deal with the celebration of Carnival around the world. Right now, the canonical work is Mikhail Bakhtin's study of the carnivalesque in the writings of François Rabelais (1968). Other important works include Victor Turner's study of Carnival in Rio (1983), Maria Goldwasser's essay in the *Encyclopedia of Religion* (1987), and Roberto DaMatta's many works on Carnival in Brazil (see especially 1991). A book of exceptional photographs of Carnival celebrations in several places around the world (Rio, New Orleans, Mexico, Germany, France, Switzerland) is Alexander Orloff's *Carnival: Myth and Cult* (1981). The text is not very sophisticated, but the photographs are wonderful. A book that captures the feel of Carnival, especially the out-of-control, ecstatic flow of the event, is journalist Alma Guillermoprieto's *Samba* (1990). Other important works include Abner Cohen on the politics of a carnival in London (1980), Julie Taylor on aesthetic debate of Carnival in Brazil (1982), and Frank Manning on Carnival in Antigua, New York, and Toronto (1978, 1988). John Fiske has some interesting observations on the place of the body in carnivalesque pleasures in popular culture (1989). I have written about the transformation of Carnival in Caracas at the end of the nineteenth century (Lavenda 1980a, 1980b). A recent work on a carnivalesque American celebration is Jack Kugelmass's study of the Greenwich Village Halloween Parade (1991). José Limón discusses the carnivalesque and narrative discourse in south Texas (1989).

Festival History in Minnesota

The historical literature on Minnesota festivals is not plentiful. There are newspaper reports, on which I have heavily relied, as well as occasional books of community history that may have some discussion of festivals. I found Blanche Zellmer, Carol Fried, and Susan Augst's study of Montgomery to be helpful, particularly concerning Kolacky Days (1976). The WPA *Guide to Minnesota,* published originally in 1938 and reprinted by the Minnesota Historical Society Press in 1985, briefly touches on some elements of Minnesota community festival life.

Growing Up: Rites of Passage, Queen Pageants, and the Upper Midwest

Scholarly literature on queen pageants is, perhaps surprisingly, almost nonexistent. At the 1993 annual meetings of the American Anthropological Association, a session entitled "Pageants and Power: Beauty and the Structuring of Value and Difference" dealt principally with queen pageants outside the United States, and has subsequently been published as *Beauty Queens on the Global Stage: Gender, Contests, and Power* (Cohen, Wilk, and Stoeltje, 1996). Prior to the publication of this collection, there was, in effect, no scholarly literature on national- or regional-level pageants. This volume is now the starting point for further research on the topic. For essays about national pageants, see A. C. Riverol (1983) and Gerald Early (1984). Note that these are not scholarly works but reflections by scholars on Miss America. Beverly Stoeltje and I seem to be the only scholars writing about queen pageants at the community level. See, e.g., Stoeltje 1987a, 1987b, 1988, 1996; Lavenda 1987, 1988, 1991a, 1992a, 1992b, 1993, 1996; and Lavenda et al. 1984. Some important works deal with issues connected with queen pageants, however. Ivan Karp's study of why Iteso women in Kenya find marriage ceremonies funny speaks to the issues of social reproduction and irony in small-town queen pageants (1989), an issue that I have developed elsewhere (1991b). Issues of domination in queen pageants and the contrast with sports are discussed by Susan Brownmiller in the context of a study of femininity (1984). An important analysis of domination, crying, and power that is directly relevant to queen pageants in Minnesota is found in Hélène Cixous and Catherine Clément (1986).

On the subject of rites of passage more generally, the standard classic source is Arnold Van Gennep (1960). Turner (1969) is the most important modern discussion of rites of passage, particularly the transitional, or liminal, period. W. Robertson Smith's classic work on ancient Arabian religion is the source for the assertion that once enemies have eaten together, they can no longer be enemies (1956). While there are many personal reminiscences on growing up and living in small towns in the Middle West, I have found essays by Carol Bly (1981) and Kathleen Norris (1993) particularly valuable.

WORKS CITED

Abrahams, Roger
    1985   An American Vocabulary of Celebrations. In *Time Out of Time: Essays on the Festival*. Ed. Alessandro Falassi. Albuquerque: University of New Mexico Press.

Abrahams, Roger, and Richard Bauman
    1978   Ranges of Festival Behavior. In *The Reversible World*. Ed. Barbara Babcock. Ithaca, N.Y.: Cornell University Press.

Anderson, Benedict
    1983   *Imagined Communities*. London: Verso.

Bakhtin, Mikhail
    1968   *Rabelais and His World*. Trans. Hélène Iswolsky. Cambridge, Mass.: MIT Press.

Bly, Carol
    1981   *Letters from the Country*. New York: Harper & Row.

Booth, Wayne
    1974   *A Rhetoric of Irony*. Chicago: University of Chicago Press.

Brownmiller, Susan
    1984   *Femininity*. New York: Simon & Schuster, Linden Press.

Buechler, Hans
    1980   *The Masked Media*. The Hague: Mouton.

Chaney, David
    1993   *Fictions of Collective Life: Public Drama in Late Modern Culture*. London: Routledge.

Cixous, Hélène, and Catherine Clément
    1986   *The Newly Born Woman.* (*La Jeune Née* [1975]). Trans. Betsy
                    Wing. Minneapolis: University of Minnesota Press.

Cohen, Abner
    1980   Drama and Politics in the Development of a London Carnival.
                    Man 15 (1): 65–87.

Cohen, Colleen Ballerino, Richard Wilk, and Beverly Stoeltje
    1996   *Beauty Queens on the Global Stage: Gender, Contests, and Power.*
                    London: Routledge.

Connerton, Paul
    1989   *How Societies Remember.* Cambridge: Cambridge University Press.

DaMatta, Roberto
    1991   Carnival, Rogues, and Heroes: An Interpretation of the Brazilian
                    Dilemma. (*Carnavais, malandros e heróis* [1979]). Trans. John
                    Drury. South Bend, Ind.: University of Notre Dame Press.

Dewey, John
    1966   *Democracy and Education: An Introduction to the Philosophy of
                    Education.* New York: Free.

Dorst, John
    1989   *The Written Suburb: An American Site, an Ethnographic Dilemma.*
                    Philadelphia: University of Pennsylvania Press.

Early, Gerald
    1984   Waiting for Miss America. *Antioch Review* 42 (3): 291–305.

Errington, Frederick
    1987   Reflexivity Deflected: The Festival of Nations as an American
                    Cultural Performance. *American Ethnologist* 14 (4): 654–667.
    1990   The Rock Creek Rodeo: Excess and Constraint in Men's Lives.
                    American Ethnologist 17 (4): 628–645.

Esman, Marjorie R.
    1982   Festivals, Change, and Unity: The Celebration of Ethnic Identity
                    among Louisiana Cajuns. *Anthropological Quarterly* 44 (5):
                    199–210.

Falassi, Alessandro
    1987   Festival: Definition and Morphology. In *Time Out of Time: Essays
                    on the Festival.* Ed. Alessandro Falassi. Albuquerque: University of
                    New Mexico Press.

Farber, Carole
    1983   High, Healthy, and Happy: Ontario Mythology on Parade. In
                    *The Celebration of Society: Perspectives on Contemporary Cultural
                    Performance.* Ed. Frank Manning. Culture and Performance. Bowl-
                    ing Green, Ohio: Bowling Green University Popular Press.

Fernandez, James
    1986   *Persuasions and Performances: The Play of Tropes in Culture.*
                    Bloomington: Indiana University Press.

Fiske, John
    1989   *Understanding Popular Culture*. Boston: Unwin Hyman.

Frankenberg, Ronald
    1957   *Village on the Border: A Study of Religion, Politics, and Football in a North Wales Community*. Prospect Heights, Ill.: Waveland.

Geertz, Clifford
    1972   Deep Play: Notes on the Balinese Cockfight. *Daedalus* 101: 1–37.
    1973   *The Interpretation of Cultures: Selected Essays*. New York: Basic Books.
    1983   *Local Knowledge: Further Essays in Interpretive Anthropology*. New York: Basic Books.

Goldwasser, Maria
    1987   Carnival. In *Encyclopedia of Religion*. Vol. 2. New York: Macmillan.

Grimes, Ronald
    1976   *Symbol and Conquest: Public Ritual and Drama in Santa Fe, New Mexico*. Ithaca, N.Y.: Cornell University Press.

Guillermoprieto, Alma
    1990   *Samba*. New York: Vintage, Vintage Departures.

Halbwachs, Maurice
    1980   *The Collective Memory*. New York: Harper & Row.

Handelman, Don
    1990   *Models and Mirrors: Towards an Anthropology of Public Events*. Cambridge: Cambridge University Press.
    1992   Passages to Play: Paradox and Process. *Play and Culture* 5 (1): 1–19.

Harvey, Thomas
    1989   Small-Town Minnesota. In *Minnesota in a Century of Change: The State and Its People Since 1900*. Ed. Clifford Clark Jr. St. Paul: Minnesota Historical Society Press.

Hobsbawm, Eric
    1983a   Introduction: Inventing Traditions. In *The Invention of Tradition*. Ed. Eric Hobsbawm and Terence Ranger. Cambridge: Cambridge University Press.
    1983b   Mass-producing Traditions: Europe, 1870–1914. In *The Invention of Tradition*. Ed. Eric Hobsbawm and Terence Ranger. Cambridge: Cambridge University Press.

Hobsbawm, Eric, and Terence Ranger, eds.
    1983   *The Invention of Tradition*. Cambridge: Cambridge University Press.

Kaplan, Anne R., Marjorie A. Hoover, and Willard B. Moore
    1986   *The Minnesota Ethnic Food Book*. St. Paul: Minnesota Historical Society Press.

Karp, Ivan
    1989   Laughter at Marriage: Subversion in Performance. In *Transformations of African Marriage*. Ed. David Parkin and David Nyamwaya. Manchester, England: Mancester University for the International African Institute.

Keillor, Garrison
    1985   *Lake Wobegon Days.* New York: Viking.
    1987   *Leaving Home.* New York: Viking.

Kugelmass, Jack
    1991   Wishes Come True: Designing the Greenwich Village Halloween Parade. *Journal of American Folklore* 104 (414): 443–465.
    1992   The Rites of the Tribe: American Jewish Tourism in Poland. In *Museums and Communities: The Politics of Public Culture*. Ed. Ivan Karp, Christine Mullen Kreamer, and Steven D. Lavine. Washington, D.C.: Smithsonian Institution Press.

Lavenda, Robert H.
    1980a   The Festival of Progress: The Globalizing World-System and the Transformation of the Caracas Carnival. *Journal of Popular Culture* 14 (3): 465–475.
    1980b   From Festival of Progress to Masque of Degradation: Carnival in Caracas as a Changing Metaphor for Social Reality. In *Play and Culture*. Ed. Helen Schwartzman. West Point, N.Y.: Leisure.
    1987   Initiation through Play: The Cultivation of Sociability in Minnesota Queen Pageants. Paper presented at Annual Meetings of the Association for the Study of Play, Montreal.
    1988   Minnesota Queen Pageants: Play, Fun, and Dead Seriousness in a Festive Mode. *Journal of American Folklore* 101: 168–175.
    1991a   Community Festivals, Paradox, and the Manipulation of Uncertainty. *Play and Culture* 4 (2): 153–168.
    1991b   Tears at the Coronation: The Limits of Play in a Playful Public Ritual. Paper presented at the Annual Meetings of the Association for the Study of Play, Charleston, S.C.
    1992a   Festivals and the Creation of Public Culture: Whose Voice(s). In *Museums and Communities: The Politics of Public Culture*. Ed. Ivan Karp, Christine Mullen Kreamer, and Steven D. Lavine. Washington, D.C.: Smithsonian Institution Press.
    1992b   Response to Handelman. *Play and Culture* 5 (1): 22–24.
    1993   The Traces of Play: TASP Presidential Address, 1992. *Journal of Play Theory and Research* 1 (1): iii–vii.
    1996   "It's Not a Beauty Pageant!": Hybrid Ideology in Minnesota Community Queen Pageants. In *Beauty Queens on the Global Stage: Gender, Contests, and Power*. Ed. Colleen Ballerino Cohen, Richard Wilk, and Beverly Stoeltje. London: Routledge.

Lavenda, Robert H., Kevin Gwost, Mark Lauer, Christopher Nelson, and JacLyn Norwood
    1984   Festivals and the Organization of Meaning: An Introduction to Community Festivals in Minnesota. In *The Masks of Play*. Ed.

Brian Sutton-Smith and Diana Kelley-Byrne. West Point, N.Y.: Leisure.

Lawrence, Denise L.
1987   Rules of Misrule: Notes on the Doo Dah Parade in Pasadena. In *Time Out of Time: Essays on the Festival*. Ed. Alessandro Falassi. Albuquerque: University of New Mexico Press.

Limón, José
1989   Carne, Carnales, and the Carnivalesque: Bakhtinian Batos, Disorder, and Narrative Discourses. *American Ethnologist* 16: 471–486.

Manning, Frank
1978   Carnival in Antigua: An Indigenous Festival in a Tourist Economy. *Anthropos* 73: 191–204.
1983   Cosmos and Chaos: Celebration in the Modern World. In *The Celebration of Society: Perspectives on Contemporary Cultural Performance*. Ed. Frank Manning. Culture and Performance. Bowling Green, Ohio: Bowling Green University Popular Press.
1988   Jamming on the Parkway. Paper presented at American Anthropological Association Meetings, Phoenix.

Marcus, George, and Michael Fischer
1986   *Anthropology as Cultural Critique*. Chicago: University of Chicago Press.

Marling, Karal Ann
1984   *The Colossus of Roads: Myth and Symbol along the American Highway*. Minneapolis: University of Minnesota Press.
1989   Culture and Leisure: The "Good Life" in Minnesota. In *Minnesota in a Century of Change*. Ed. Clifford E. Clark Jr. St. Paul: Minnesota Historical Society Press.
1990   *Blue Ribbon: A Social and Pictorial History of the Minnesota State Fair*. St. Paul: Minnesota Historical Society.

Martindale, Don, and R. Galen Hanson
1969   *Small Town and the Nation: The Conflict of Local and Translocal Forces*. Westport, Conn.: Greenwood.

Marvin, Patrice Avon, and Nicholas Curchin Vrooman
1985   *Till the Cows Come Home: Being a Story of the Goodhue County Agricultural Society and Mechanics' Institute Annual Fair*. A Project of the Goodhue County Historical Society. Zumbrota, Minn.: Wings/hands.

Moore, Willard B., ed.
1989   *Circles of Tradition: Folk Arts in Minnesota*. St. Paul: Published for the University of Minnesota Art Museum by the Minnesota Historical Society Press.

Nass, David L.
1989   The Rural Experience. In *Minnesota in a Century of Change: The State and Its People Since 1900*. Ed. Clifford Clark Jr. St. Paul: Minnesota Historical Society Press.

Norris, Kathleen
1993   *Dakota: A Spiritual Geography.* New York: Ticknor & Fields.
Orloff, Alexander
1981   *Carnival: Myth and Cult.* Worgl, Austria: Verlag Perlinger.
Greta
1996   *In Search of the Corn Queen.* Introduction by Karal Ann Marling. Washington, D.C.: National Museum of American Art, Smithsonian Institution.

Prosterman, Leslie
1995   *Ordinary Life, Festival Days: Aesthetics in the Midwestern County Fair.* Washington, D.C.: Smithsonian Institution Press.

Riverol, A. C.
1983   Myth America and Other Misses: A Second Look at the American Beauty Contests. *ETC* 40 (2): 207–217.

Simmel, Georg
1950   Sociability: An Example of Pure, or Formal, Sociology. In *The Sociology of George Simmel.* Ed. and trans. K. Wolff. Glencoe, Ill.: Free Press.

Smith, Robert J.
1972   Festivals and Celebrations. In *Folklore and Folklife: An Introduction.* Ed. Richard Dorson. Chicago: University of Chicago Press.

Smith, Sheldon
1984   The Re-establishment of Community: The Emerging Festival System of the American West. *Journal of American Culture* 7: 91–100.

Smith, W. Robertson
1956   *The Religion of the Semites: The Fundamental Institutions.* [1889]. Reprint, New York: Meridian.

Stoeltje, Beverly
1983   Festival in America. In *Handbook of American Folklore.* Ed. Richard Dorson. Bloomington: Indiana University Press.
1987a   Cultural Queens: Modernization and Representation. Paper presented at Annual Meetings of the Association for the Study of Play, Montreal.
1987b   Riding, Roping, and Reunion: Cowboy Festival. In *Time Out of Time: Essays on the Festival.* Ed. Alessandro Falassi. Albuquerque, N.M.: University of New Mexico Press.
1988   Gender Representations in Performance: The Cowgirl and the Hostess. *Journal of Folklore Research* 25 (3): 219–241.
1996   The Snake Charmer Queen: Ritual, Competition, and Signification in an American Festival. In *Beauty Queens on the Global Stage: Gender, Contests, and Power.* Ed. Colleen Ballerino Cohen, Richard Wilk, and Beverly Stoeltje. London: Routledge.

Swiderski, Richard
1986   *Voices: An Anthropologist's Dialogue with an Italian American*

Festival. Culture and Performance. London, Ontario: Centre for Social and Humanistic Studies, University of Western Ontario.

Taylor, Julie
    1982   The Politics of Aesthetic Debate: The Case of Brazilian Carnival. *Ethnology* 21: 301–311.

Tomlinson, John
    1991   *Cultural Imperialism.* Baltimore: Johns Hopkins University Press.

Turner, Victor
    1969   *The Ritual Process: Structure and Anti-structure.* Symbol, Myth, and Ritual Series. Ithaca, N.Y.: Cornell University Press.
    1982   *From Ritual to Theater: The Human Seriousness of Play.* New York: Performing Arts Journal Publications.
    1983   Carnaval in Rio: Dionysian Drama in an Industrializing Society. In *The Celebration of Society: Perspectives on Contemporary Cultural Performance.* Ed. Frank Manning. Culture and Performance. Bowling Green, Ohio: Bowling Green University Popular Press.

Varenne, Hervé
    1977   *Americans Together: Structured Diversity in a Midwestern Town.* New York: Teachers College Press.

Warner, W. Lloyd
    1959   *The Living and the Dead: A Study of the Symbolic Life of Americans.* New Haven, Conn.: Yale University Press.

Works Progress Administration
    1985   *The WPA Guide to Minnesota.* [1938]. Reprint, St. Paul: Minnesota Historical Society Press.

Zellmer, Blanche, Carol Fried, and Susan Augst
    1976   *Montgomery: From the "Big Woods" to the Kolacky Capital, 1856–1976.* Montgomery, Minn.: The Committee [Montgomery Bicentennial Committee].

INDEX